Media Violence

Other Books of Related Interest:

Opposing Viewpoints Series

Sexual Violence

Violence

At Issue Series

Is Media Violence a Problem?

Should Social Networking Sites Be Banned?

Video Games

Contemporary Issues Companion

Gun Violence

Current Controversies Series

School Violence

Social Networking

"Congress shall make no law . . . abridging the freedom of speech, or of the press."

First Amendment to the U.S. Constitution

The basic foundation of our democracy is the First Amendment guarantee of freedom of expression. The Opposing Viewpoints Series is dedicated to the concept of this basic freedom and the idea that it is more important to practice it than to enshrine it.

Media Violence

David M. Haugen and Susan Musser, Book Editors

GREENHAVEN PRESS
A part of Gale, Cengage Learning

GALE
CENGAGE Learning

Detroit • New York • San Francisco • New Haven, Conn • Waterville, Maine • London

GALE
CENGAGE Learning·

Christine Nasso, *Publisher*
Elizabeth Des Chenes, *Managing Editor*

© 2009 Greenhaven Press, a part of Gale, Cengage Learning.

Gale and Greenhaven Press are registered trademarks used herein under license.

For more information, contact:
Greenhaven Press
27500 Drake Rd.
Farmington Hills, MI 48331-3535
Or you can visit our Internet site at gale.cengage.com

For product information and technology assistance, contact us at

Gale Customer Support, 1-800-877-4253
For permission to use material from this text or product, submit all requests online at
www.cengage.com/permissions

Further permissions questions can be emailed to permissionrequest@cengage.com

Articles in Greenhaven Press anthologies are often edited for length to meet page require-ments. In addition, original titles of these works are changed to clearly present the main thesis and to explicitly indicate the author's opinion. Every effort is made to ensure that Greenhaven Press accurately reflects the original intent of the authors. Every effort has been made to trace the owners of copyrighted material.

Cover photograph reproduced by permission of iStock.

LIBRARY OF CONGRESS CATALOGING-IN-PUBLICATION DATA

Media violence / David Haugen and Susan Musser, book editor.
    p. cm. -- (Opposing viewpoints)
    Includes bibliographical references and index.
    ISBN-13: 978-0-7377-4218-3 (hardcover)
    ISBN-13: 978-0-7377-4219-0 (pbk.)
    1. Violence in mass media. 2. Violence in popular culture. I. Haugen, David M.,
1969- II. Musser, Susan.
    P96.V5M426 2009
    363.3--dc22
                                        2008030355

Printed in the United States of America
1 2 3 4 5 6 7 12 11 10 09 08

Contents

Chapter 3: What Are the Effects of Violence and Suffering in News Media Reporting?

Why Consider Opposing Viewpoints?

> *"The only way in which a human being can make some approach to knowing the whole of a subject is by hearing what can be said about it by persons of every variety of opinion and studying all modes in which it can be looked at by every character of mind. No wise man ever acquired his wisdom in any mode but this."*
>
> John Stuart Mill

In our media-intensive culture it is not difficult to find differing opinions. Thousands of newspapers and magazines and dozens of radio and television talk shows resound with differing points of view. The difficulty lies in deciding which opinion to agree with and which "experts" seem the most credible. The more inundated we become with differing opinions and claims, the more essential it is to hone critical reading and thinking skills to evaluate these ideas. Opposing Viewpoints books address this problem directly by presenting stimulating debates that can be used to enhance and teach these skills. The varied opinions contained in each book examine many different aspects of a single issue. While examining these conveniently edited opposing views, readers can develop critical thinking skills such as the ability to compare and contrast authors' credibility, facts, argumentation styles, use of persuasive techniques, and other stylistic tools. In short, the Opposing Viewpoints Series is an ideal way to attain the higher-level thinking and reading skills so essential in a culture of diverse and contradictory opinions.

In addition to providing a tool for critical thinking, Opposing Viewpoints books challenge readers to question their own strongly held opinions and assumptions. Most people form their opinions on the basis of upbringing, peer pressure, and personal, cultural, or professional bias. By reading carefully balanced opposing views, readers must directly confront new ideas as well as the opinions of those with whom they disagree. This is not to simplistically argue that everyone who reads opposing views will—or should—change his or her opinion. Instead, the series enhances readers' understanding of their own views by encouraging confrontation with opposing ideas. Careful examination of others' views can lead to the readers' understanding of the logical inconsistencies in their own opinions, perspective on why they hold an opinion, and the consideration of the possibility that their opinion requires further evaluation.

Evaluating Other Opinions

To ensure that this type of examination occurs, Opposing Viewpoints books present all types of opinions. Prominent spokespeople on different sides of each issue as well as well-known professionals from many disciplines challenge the reader. An additional goal of the series is to provide a forum for other, less known, or even unpopular viewpoints. The opinion of an ordinary person who has had to make the decision to cut off life support from a terminally ill relative, for example, may be just as valuable and provide just as much insight as a medical ethicist's professional opinion. The editors have two additional purposes in including these less known views. One, the editors encourage readers to respect others' opinions—even when not enhanced by professional credibility. It is only by reading or listening to and objectively evaluating others' ideas that one can determine whether they are worthy of consideration. Two, the inclusion of such viewpoints encourages the important critical thinking skill of objectively evaluating an author's credentials and bias. This evaluation will illuminate an author's reasons for taking a particular stance on an issue and will aid in readers' evaluation of the author's ideas.

It is our hope that these books will give readers a deeper understanding of the issues debated and an appreciation of the complexity of even seemingly simple issues when good and honest people disagree. This awareness is particularly important in a democratic society such as ours in which people enter into public debate to determine the common good. Those with whom one disagrees should not be regarded as enemies but rather as people whose views deserve careful examination and may shed light on one's own.

Thomas Jefferson once said that "difference of opinion leads to inquiry, and inquiry to truth." Jefferson, a broadly educated man, argued that "if a nation expects to be ignorant and free . . . it expects what never was and never will be." As individuals and as a nation, it is imperative that we consider the opinions of others and examine them with skill and discernment. The Opposing Viewpoints Series is intended to help readers achieve this goal.

David L. Bender and Bruno Leone,
Founders

"Before age 8, children cannot discriminate between real life and fantasy. On-screen violence is as real to them as violence that they witness at home or in their community. From childhood's magical thinking and impulsive behavior, adolescents must develop abstract thought and social controls to prepare them to deal with adult realities. If this development process occurs in a violent environment, it can become distorted. Media, with which children spend more time than with parents or teachers, have great potential for shaping the hearts, minds, and behaviors of America's young people—and we need to take this potential very seriously."

American Academy of Pediatrics,
Testimony before
U.S. Commerce Committee

"The rule of the real says that however strong media influences may be, real life is stronger. Real love, real money, real political events and real-life, unmediated interpersonal experience all shape kids' lives, minds and behavior more powerfully than any entertainment products."

Maggie Cutler, The Nation

Introduction

Critics of violence in the media have long claimed a connection between what people see and hear and what behaviors they exhibit. In their complaints against excessive or graphic violence in music, film, television, books, and Internet Web sites, most concerned observers focus on the impact of violent media upon the young—those whose minds are deemed most impressionable and who supposedly lack clear distinctions between fantasy and reality. Many prestigious organizations and popular spokespersons have added their opinions and research to a growing body of findings that demonstrate links between young people's consumption of violent media and their propensity toward aggression. In addition, every media outlet has been scrutinized and held accountable for exploiting—if not directly marketing to—youthful audiences by inundating them with violent messages and images.

In 2005 the American Psychological Association (APA) called upon the video game industry to curb violent content in its products to allay detrimental effects on children. The APA was most disturbed that nearly three-quarters of violent behavior in games goes unpunished or lacks moral consequence. Elizabeth Carll, cochair of the APA Committee on Violence in Video Games and Interactive Media, said in a prepared statement, "Showing violent acts without consequences teaches youth that violence is an effective means of resolving conflict. Whereas, seeing pain and suffering as a consequence can inhibit aggressive behavior." The Parents Television Council (PTC) has sounded a similar note about the effects of television violence on young people. In 2007 the PTC released a report asserting that the amount of onscreen violence in prime-time programming had risen 75 percent since 1998. The PTC expressed its irritation that broadcasters would choose to increase violent programming "despite overwhelming evidence pointing to a direct and causal relationship between violent entertainment products and aggressive behavior in children."

While media violence watchdogs quite commonly target video games and television, recently they have also accused rap music and movies of contributing to the glorification of violence in youth culture. In decades past, comic books and heavy metal music were added to the list of pop culture arti- facts supposedly promoting delinquency and aggression. Yet despite the outcry, the finger-pointing, and the evidence draw- ing connections between fictionalized violence and real-world violence, defenders of the media believe these forms of ex- pression are unfairly targeted. Most of these media champions agree that portrayals of violence are becoming more graphic and explicit, but all seem to contend that any restriction would be an infringement on the First Amendment right to free speech. In a joint statement concerning violence in the media, the American Library Association (ALA) and affiliate organi- zations maintain, "The root causes of violence in society lie beyond violent portrayals by the media. This being so, the search for solutions must go beyond facile censorship initia- tives, which inevitably compromise our fundamental freedom of expression, and instead seek out and attack these root causes."

In addition to guarding freedom of expression, most advo- cates claim that the media (usually the medium with which the spokesperson shares a connection) serve as scapegoats for much deeper problems in society. Jib Fowles, a professor of communications, explained why television makes such a fa- vored whipping boy.

> First, it is a large target, present in one form or another in virtually every household in America. Second, if one puts on blinders, there might seem to be some correspondence be- tween the mayhem on the television screen and real-life ag- gression; both televised entertainment and the real world deal in hostilities. Third and most important, television vio- lence attracts no champions; the very idea of defending it seems silly to most people. Even industry representatives rarely get beyond conciliatory statements when they are compelled to address the matter. In one survey, 78 percent

of entertainment industry executives expressed concern about the content of the action dramas they helped produce.

Fowles takes the view that crusades against television violence are really expressions of other contests of wills—between the old and the young, between the weak and the strong, and even between the upper classes and the lower classes. "Whatever its immediate source," Fowles writes, "the energy that breathes life into the whipping boy of television violence has its ultimate origins in fear—fear of disorder that, in the extreme, could overturn society." Those with less lofty analyses most often contend that the media are only part of a person's environment; even the APA—which holds media violence to account—has avowed that a child's native temperament, impaired mental health, instances of parental abuse or neglect, poverty, and lack of strong role models are contributing factors to the problem of youth violence.

Critics of media violence, however, argue that as long as violent content promotes aggression—especially in children—then the media should take steps to regulate the amount of violent programming that reaches young viewers. According to a *Time* magazine poll in 2005, just over half of respondents supported empowering the Federal Communications Commission (FCC) to place tighter controls on the broadcasting of adult content. Censorship of any kind, however, is not a popular remedy. Congressional bills granting the FCC power to regulate television violence, for example, have routinely stalled on Capitol Hill. Yet the clash between First Amendment freedoms and the argument that media violence is a negative influence on society continues while concerned individuals and organizations proffer solutions.

Elizabeth Thoman, founder of the Center for Media Literacy, does not deny the value of freedom of expression, but she insists that preserving the health of society is of paramount importance. "Of course, our First Amendment protections are still important. But so are the thousands of lives being lost every year. The issue, I believe, is no longer one of protecting free speech but of protecting human life; it is not a question of censoring ideas but of changing behaviors that are endangering the health and safety of every citizen, young and old." Her organization advocates the teaching of media literacy to all people—especially the young—so that everyone will have the skills necessary to understand and analyze the messages transmitted by the media. In this way, Thoman and the Center for Media Literacy hope that audiences will discern the role that violence plays in media storytelling and be able to critically reflect on what they see, hear, and read. The center also believes that empowering parents to become media literate will give them the tools they need to discuss media violence with their children and structure an environment that limits children's exposure to material that is unsuitable for their age.

Those who oppose government restriction on the media have always assumed that parents are and should remain the ones who control media access for their children. *San Francisco Chronicle* television critic Tim Goodman has argued that parents need to take greater responsibility for their children's television viewing habits. Pressuring government to act, he attests, is simply an example of how lazy many parents are when ratings systems and program-blocking tools are already in place. "To whine about how Hollywood should tone it down ... completely misses the point about whose kid it is," Goodman writes in an article he succinctly titled "Hate Violence? Turn It Off." He encourages parents to "vote with your remote" and either watch channels with limited violence or turn off objectionable programming altogether. Similarly, other commentators like Goodman have argued that parents have the power to keep their children from objectionable material—whether it be music, films, or Internet sites; they just need to exercise that authority and make clear rules.

Government regulation, education, and relying on parental oversight are three commonly ascribed methods to address the growing concern over media violence. In *Opposing Viewpoints: Media Violence*, various commentators debate some of these possible remedies as well as broaden the discussion to look at other facets of the issue. In chapters titled "Is Media Violence a Serious Problem?," "How Should Media Violence Be Regulated?," "What Are the Effects of Violence and Suffering in News Media Reporting?," and "Is the Internet a New Medium for Violence?," government organizations, lawyers, journalists, and other concerned parties offer differing opinions on whether violence in the media signals a coarsening of American culture or whether, as Tim Goodman states, the excessive browbeating of media for their portrayals of violence "is to put our heads in the sand about the world we live in."

OPPOSING
VIEWPOINTS®
SERIES

CHAPTER 1

Is Media Violence a Serious Problem?

Chapter Preface

In September 2007 members of Congress held hearings in which they questioned representatives of the recording and video industry about whether certain strains of hip-hop music promote violence and sexism. Specifically, the lawmakers were concerned that the industry is exploiting controversial messages for profit and failing to do enough to help keep mature, often graphic, content away from impressionable children. U.S. representative Bobby L. Rush affirmed that the hearings were not about finger-pointing or limiting artistic freedom; instead he spoke of an overall culture of violence that has "reduced too many of our youngsters to automatons, those who don't recognize life, those who don't value life." Rush and colleagues asked the assembled industry leaders if they would accept a voluntary ban on specific language that some might consider offensive in rap lyrics.

Most of the executives regretted the fact that America's young people were awash in a culture of violence but denied that curtailing free speech would do much to resolve that problem. Edgar Bronfman Jr., chairman of the Warner Music Group, added that it would be impossible to dictate taste and to collectively agree which language to ban. Some of the rap artists present at the hearings resented the fact that hip hop had become a scapegoat for violence because, in their view, the music merely reflected the violent lifestyle that is commonplace in America's economically depressed communities. However, according to the *New York Times*, which reported on the hearings, one artist accepted the blame for contributing to the culture of violence. Percy Miller—known to the hip-hop world as Master P—said that he and other hip-hop artists were "inflaming this problem by not being responsible" for the messages that reach young people.

Whether the lyrics of rap songs are responsible for inflaming violent or sexist behavior is still a matter of debate. In 2003 an Emory University study of 522 black girls between the ages of fourteen and eighteen from nonurban, lower class neighborhoods in Birmingham, Alabama, found that those who watched at least fourteen hours of "gangsta rap" videos per week were more likely to engage in violent acts than their peers who rarely watched such videos. The findings showed that video-watching girls were three times more likely to hit a teacher and over two-and-a-half times more likely to get arrested than their peers. Then, in a 2006 study conducted by the Pacific Institute for Research and Evaluation, the survey responses of one thousand community college students between the ages of fifteen and twenty-five led researchers to the conclusion that rap music was "consistently associated" with alcohol-related disorders, drug use, and violence.

Critics, however, continually note that the link between media violence—including the violent content of rap music—and real-world violence is unproven. Jonathan Freedman, a psychology professor at the University of Toronto, contends, "If exposure to violent media causes aggression and violent behavior, one would surely expect the rate of violent crime to have gone through the roof. Yet, since 1992 there has been a dramatic drop in violent crime, including violent crime committed by young males [the primary target of studies linking media violence and real violence]." Hip-hop artist David Banner—one of the performers who spoke at the congressional hearings in 2007—argued that listening to rap music as a youngster often sublimated his own feelings of rage and kept him from acting out his anger. Banner also noted that "drugs, violence, and the criminal element were around long before hip hop existed," and therefore silencing hip hop would have no effect on these ever-present problems of society.

In the following chapter, media pundits and analysts expand this debate into other forms of media commonly maligned for contributing to a violent society in America.

> *"Media violence poses a threat to public health inasmuch as it leads to an increase in real-world violence and aggression."*

Exposure to Violence in the Media Leads to Violent Behavior

L. Rowell Huesmann and Laramie D. Taylor

In the following viewpoint, L. Rowell Huesmann and Laramie D. Taylor argue that the portrayal of violence in all forms of media negatively impacts American society—and especially the nation's youth—because individuals who are exposed to violence in the media are more likely to commit violent or aggressive acts. While the authors concede that other risk factors can lead an individual to become violent, they maintain that the repetition of violence in the media can desensitize viewers to its real-world consequences, and the way in which it is justified in narratives can lead young people to view violence as an acceptable solution to problems. L. Rowell Huesmann is a professor of communication studies and psychology at the University of Michigan, and

L. Rowell Huesmann and Laramie D. Taylor, "The Role of Media Violence in Violent Behavior," *Annual Review of Public Health*, vol. 27, 2006, pp. 393–415. Copyright © 2006 by Annual Reviews Inc. All rights reserved. Reproduced by permission.

Laramie D. Taylor is an assistant professor of communications at the University of California at Davis. Both have written extensively on the affects of exposure to media violence.

As you read, consider the following questions:

1. According to Huesmann and Taylor, why is it necessary to take a developmental perspective when examining the correlation between media violence and aggression or violence?

2. In the authors' view, how does desensitization to media violence make proactive aggression more likely in children?

3. Based on the authors' assessment, how does the statistical correlation between media violence and aggression compare with the correlations between other behaviors and health risks?

One of the notable changes in our social environment in the twentieth century is the advent and saturation of mass media. In this new environment, radio, television, movies, videos, video games, and computer networks have assumed central roles in our daily lives. For better or for worse, the mass media are having an enormous impact on our values, beliefs, and behaviors. Unfortunately, the consequences of one particular element of the mass media exposure has particularly detrimental effects on viewers' and others' health. Research evidence has accumulated over many years that exposure to violence on television and in video games increases the risk of violent behavior on the viewer's part just as growing up in an environment filled with real violence increases the risk of violent behavior. . . .

Taking a Multifaceted Approach

Before reviewing the research literature, however, we must emphasize several points. First, the weight of the evidence indicates that violent actions seldom result from a single cause;

rather, multiple factors converging over time contribute to such behavior. Accordingly, the influence of the violent mass media is best viewed as one of the many potential factors that influence the risk for violence. No reputable researcher is suggesting that media violence is "the" cause of violent behavior.

Second, a developmental perspective [an approach that examines human psychological changes as an individual ages] is essential to an adequate understanding of how media violence affects youthful conduct and to the formulation of a coherent public health response to this problem. Most youth who are aggressive and engage in some forms of antisocial behavior do not go on to become violent teens and adults. Still, research has shown that a significant proportion of aggressive children are likely to grow up to be aggressive adults and that seriously violent adolescents and adults were often highly aggressive and even violent as children. The best single predictor of violent behavior in older adolescents, young adults, and even middle-aged adults is the occurrence of aggressive behavior in childhood. Thus, influences, such as exposure to media violence, that promote aggressive behavior in young children can contribute to increasingly aggressive and ultimately violent behavior many years later.

Third, it is important to avoid the error of assuming that small statistical effects necessarily translate into small practical or public health effects. There are many circumstances in which statistically small effects have large practical consequences, especially when small effects accumulate over time and over large proportions of the relevant population. With such accumulation, even small statistical effects of media violence on aggressive behavior can have important social consequences. Many medical scientists have avoided the problem of underestimating the public health importance of small effects by translating their findings into death rates for the entire U.S. population, but behavioral scientists have not traditionally done this type of population-rate translation. Thus, people are frequently shocked to learn that the effects of some environmental contaminants on behavior and mental health can be as large or larger than the effects of other contaminants on physical health.

Finally, the case against media violence, like the case against other potential public health threats, must be made by integrating the evidence from multiple approaches to research. Cross-sectional survey studies in which the amount of media violence to which a person is exposed is correlated with their propensity to behave aggressively have high external validity in determining whether exposure to violence and violent behavior are related, but they say little about the causal process involved. True experiments, in which participants are randomly assigned to conditions experiencing different doses of violence, provide the best evidence for causation, but they often lack external validity or generalizability. However, out of ethical necessity, these experiments generally have not examined effects of the most serious types of physical aggression and have not examined the long-term effects of exposure to violence. Longitudinal studies can test in an externally valid manner whether long-term exposure to violence has effects, whether childhood exposure is related to adult aggression, and whether it is more plausible to believe that violent behavior stimulates exposure to violence or that exposure to violence stimulates violent behavior. All three types of research should be integrated in reaching any conclusion.

Assessing the Severity of Violent Behaviors

Before proceeding, it is important to define two terms clearly: media violence and violent behavior. Different people have used different definitions of these terms at different times. For this review, we define media violence as visual portrayals of acts of physical aggression by one human against another. This definition of media violence does not include off-screen poisonings that might be implied, but rather it refers to visually portrayed physically aggressive acts by one person against another. This definition has evolved as theories about the effects of media violence have evolved and represents an attempt to describe the kind of violent media presentation that is most likely to teach the viewer to be more violent. Movies and programs depicting violence of this type were common 20 years ago, and they are common now: *Dirty Harry, The Godfather, Mad Max, Cliffhanger, True Lies, Pulp Fiction, Kill Bill,* etc. The list is endless.

The definition adopted for violent behavior can also be important for how the empirical research is interpreted. Most researchers studying media effects on behavior have focused on what they call aggressive behavior. The accepted definition states that aggressive behavior refers to an act intended to injure or irritate another person. The act could be physical or nonphysical. This includes many kinds of behavior that do not seem to fit the commonly understood meaning of violence. Hurling insults and spreading harmful rumors fit the definition. Of course, the aggressive behaviors of greatest concern to society clearly involve physical aggression. However, physical aggression may range in severity from acts such as pushing or shoving to more serious physical assaults and fighting, even extending to violent acts that carry a significant risk of serious injury. We use the term violent behavior in this review to describe more serious forms of physical aggression that pose a significant risk of serious injury to victims.

Violent and aggressive behaviors are best viewed as falling on a continuum of severity. As described above, a very strong correlation exists between mildly aggressive behavior and the risk for seriously aggressive or violent behavior later in life. Furthermore, significant evidence suggests that the display of aggressive thinking or aggressive emotions is a valid predictor of risk for violence. Consequently, studies investigating any of these types of aggression can be valuable. . . .

Priming Violence in the Short Term

Most theorists would now agree that the short-term effects of exposure to media violence are mostly due to (*a*) priming processes, (*b*) excitation processes, and (*c*) the immediate imitation of specific behaviors. Priming is the process through which spreading activation in the brain's neural network from the locus representing an external observed stimulus excites another brain node representing a cognition, emotion, or behavior. The external stimulus can be inherently linked to a cognition, e.g., the sight of a gun is inherently linked to the concept of aggression, or the external stimulus can be something inherently neutral like a particular ethnic group (e.g., African Americans) that has become linked in the past to certain beliefs or behaviors (e.g., welfare). The primed concepts make behaviors linked to them more likely. When media violence primes aggressive concepts, aggression is more likely.

To the extent that mass media presentations arouse the observer, aggressive behavior may also become more likely in the short run for two possible reasons: excitation transfer and general arousal. First, a subsequent stimulus that arouses an emotion (e.g., a provocation arousing anger) may be perceived as more severe than it is because some of the emotional response stimulated by the media presentation is misattributed as due to the provocation transfer. For example, immediately following an exciting media presentation, such excitation transfer could cause more aggressive responses to provocation. Alternatively, the increased general arousal stimulated by the media presentation may simply reach such a peak that inhibition of inappropriate responses is diminished, and dominant learned responses are displayed in social problem solving, e.g., direct instrumental aggression.

The third short-term process, imitation of specific behaviors, can be viewed as a special case of the more general long-term process of observational learning. In recent years, evidence has accumulated that human and primate young have an innate tendency to imitate whomever they observe. Observation of specific social behaviors around them increases the likelihood of children behaving exactly that way. As children observe violent behavior, they are prone to imitate it.

Effects of Repeated Exposure over Time

Long-term content effects, in contrast, seem to be due to (*a*) more lasting observational learning of cognitions and behaviors and (*b*) activation and desensitization of emotional processes. According to social cognitive models, observational learning influences behavior not only in the short term after a behavior is observed but also in the long term. The social scripts acquired through observation of family, peers, community, and mass media become more complex, abstracted, and automatic in their invocation. During this period, children's social cognitive schemas about the world around them are also elaborated. For example, extensive observation of violence has been shown to bias children's world schemas toward attributing hostility to others' actions. Such attributions in turn increase the likelihood of children behaving aggressively. As children mature further, normative beliefs about which social behaviors are appropriate become crystallized and begin to act as filters to limit inappropriate social behaviors. These normative beliefs are influenced in part by children's observation of the behaviors of those around them including behaviors observed in the mass media.

Long-term socialization effects of the mass media are also increased quite likely by the way the mass media and video games affect emotions. Through classical conditioning, fear, anger, or general arousal can become linked with specific stimuli after only a few exposures. These emotions influence behavior in social settings away from the media source through stimulus generalization. A child may then react with inappropriate anger or fear in a novel situation similar to one that the child has observed in the media.

At the same time, repeated exposures to emotionally activating media or video games can lead to habituation of certain natural emotional reactions, or "desensitization." Behaviors observed by the child viewer that might seem unusual at first start to seem more normative after the behaviors are viewed many times. Emotions experienced automatically by child viewers in response to a particular scene decline in intensity after many exposures. For example, most humans seem to have an innate negative emotional response to observing blood, gore, and violence.

Increased heart rates, perspiration, and self-reports of discomfort often accompany such exposure. However, with repeated exposure to violence, this negative emotional response habituates, and the child becomes desensitized. The child can then think about and plan proactive aggressive acts without experiencing negative affect. Consequently, proactive aggression becomes more likely. The body of research on observational learning shows that scripts, world schemas, and normative beliefs about behaviors can all be acquired from observations without viewer awareness and with little effortful cognition. Similarly, desensitization of emotional responding does not require effortful cognition. One of the insidious facts about socialization by the mass media is that much of the socialization process happens without children being aware of what is happening.

The Lure of Violent Media

Obviously, not all observers of violence are affected equally at all times by what they observe. Research has shown that the effects of media violence on children are moderated by situational characteristics of the presentation, including how well it attracts and sustains attention, personal characteristics of the viewer including one's own aggressive predispositions, and characteristics of the physical and human context in which the children are exposed to violence. Of course, these factors

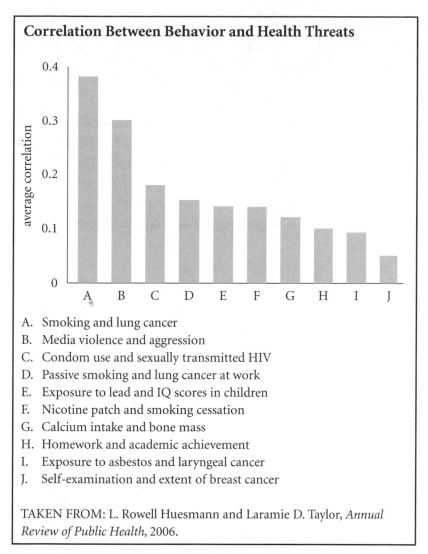

Correlation Between Behavior and Health Threats

average correlation

A. Smoking and lung cancer
B. Media violence and aggression
C. Condom use and sexually transmitted HIV
D. Passive smoking and lung cancer at work
E. Exposure to lead and IQ scores in children
F. Nicotine patch and smoking cessation
G. Calcium intake and bone mass
H. Homework and academic achievement
I. Exposure to asbestos and laryngeal cancer
J. Self-examination and extent of breast cancer

TAKEN FROM: L. Rowell Huesmann and Laramie D. Taylor, *Annual Review of Public Health*, 2006.

all interact with each other. For example, how realistic a violent scene will seem to a child depends on the form and content of the scene, the child's experiences and propensities to accept what one sees, and probably other viewers present when the child observes the scene.

Presentations that do not attract a minimum level of attention will have little influence on a child. Although effects can occur through peripheral processing without cognitive resources being devoted to processing the material in a presentation, they cannot occur without a minimum level of viewer attention. Consequently, form and content factors that attract children's attention are very important in determining the magnitude of effects that presentations will have. Factors that facilitate attention in young children appear to include rapid movement, bright colors, and loud noises, traits often characteristic of violent scenes. Of course, video games inherently combine these form elements with demands on cognitive resources, whereas TV programs and movies vary more on this dimension.

Even if a scene grabs a child's attention, not all violent portrayals pose the same risk to viewers. A variety of studies—primarily laboratory investigations involving children and young adults—indicate that how violence or aggression is presented can alter its meaning for the audience and may moderate viewers' behavioral, cognitive, and emotional reactions.

Justification and Realism Promote Imitation

According to observational-learning theory, when violence is portrayed as justified, viewers are likely to come to believe that their own aggressive responses to a perceived offense are also appropriate, so they are therefore more apt to behave aggressively. Findings from experiments that varied the extent to which the observed violence was justified have demonstrated that seemingly warranted media violence indeed increases aggression. Theoretically, rewarding perpetrators for their aggression should also raise the likelihood that viewers will model the aggressive act, and indeed, media portrayals in which violence is rewarded have increased the risk that viewers will behave aggressively. Nor is an explicit reward necessary; seeing unpunished media violence may also enhance learning of aggressive thoughts and behaviors.

Although explicit portrayal of blood, gore, or other painful consequences might be expected to dissuade viewers from aggression, research has generally suggested that such portrayals may increase aggressiveness on the part of the viewer. Repeated exposure to such negative consequences can lead to desensitization to future scenes of blood and gore and to pain expressed by victims. Such habituation may effectively remove the punishing nature of consequences of media aggression. Empirically, viewers who show less negative emotional reactions to viewing violence are more likely to behave aggressively than those who show more negative reactions.

Observational-learning theory suggests that children who identify fairly strongly with an aggressive character or perceive a violent scene as realistic are especially likely to have aggressive ideas primed by the observed violence, to imitate the character, or to acquire a variety of aggressive scripts and schemas. When people are led to identify with a character by imagining themselves as the protagonist in a violent film, the aggression-inducing effects of viewing the film are enhanced. Viewers are more likely to identify with and be influenced by an aggressive character portrayed as similar to themselves (e.g., in age, gender, and race). However, the perpetrator's overall attractiveness, power, and charisma may be more important than any of these personal attributes by themselves. For example, in the early 1970s, African American children imitated the behavior of White male actors more than African American actors.

Also, realistic portrayals are more likely to increase viewers' aggression than those presented in a more fictionalized or fantastic fashion. In longitudinal research, Huesmann and colleagues found that children who thought that violent shows they watched were telling about life "just like it really is" or who identified with aggressive TV characters had relatively high average scores on a measure of physical and verbal aggression one year later and scored higher on a composite measure of (physical, verbal and indirect, or relational) aggressiveness 15 years later. Those most at risk to behave aggressively were males who both watched violence and identified with violent characters. For those who already have a well-developed conception of the world around them as nonviolent, material that contrasts too much with their existing conception will have less effect than will material that they can assimilate into their world schemas. . . .

Similarities Between Media Violence and Smoking

This review has presented compelling evidence that short-term exposure to media violence stimulates more aggressive and violent behavior in the young viewer immediately and that long-term exposure leads to the acquisition of social cognitions (scripts, world schemas, attitudes, and beliefs) that increase the risk of aggressive and violent behavior in the observers of media violence beyond childhood. The psychological processes through which this happens are well understood by researchers. Many within-person and within-situation factors that exacerbate or mitigate this effect have been identified. However, one valid remaining question would be whether the size of this effect is large enough that one should consider it a public health threat.

We argue that the answer is yes. We base this argument on two calculations. First, according to the best meta-analyses, the long-term size of the effect of exposure to media violence in childhood on later aggressive or violent behavior is about equivalent to a correlation of 0.20 to 0.30. Although some researchers may argue that this explains only 4%–9% of the individual variation in aggressive behavior, as several scholars have pointed out, percent variance explained is not a good statistic to use when predicting low probability events with high social costs. After all, effects of such size can have real social significance. As Rosenthal has pointed out, a correlation of 0.3 with aggression translates into a change in the odds of aggression from 50/50 to 65/35—not a trivial change when one is dealing with life-threatening behavior. Moreover, the relation is highly replicable even across researchers who disagree about the reasons and across countries.

Second, one should compare the size of the effects of media violence on public health with that of other recognized threats. . . . The average obtained correlation for the relation between exposure to media violence and aggression is compared with the average correlation between smoking and lung cancer, condom use and sexually transmitted HIV, exposure to lead and IQ scores, exposure to asbestos and laryngeal cancer, and many others. . . . The average obtained correlation between exposure to media violence and aggression is greater than all the others except the correlation between smoking and lung cancer. If the other correlations displayed are large enough for us to consider those environmental pollutants as threats to public health, we should also consider media violence a threat to public health.

Perhaps one of the best parallels is the relation between smoking and lung cancer. Not everyone who smokes gets lung cancer, and not everyone who gets lung cancer was a smoker. Smoking is not the only factor that causes lung cancer, but it is an important factor. Similarly, not everyone who watches violent television becomes aggressive, and not everyone who is aggressive watches violent television. Watching violent TV programs is not the only factor that causes aggression, but it is an important factor.

Media violence poses a threat to public health inasmuch as it leads to an increase in real-world violence and aggression. Research clearly shows that fictional television and film violence contribute to an increase in aggression and violence, both in the short term and across the life span. Television news violence also contributes to increased violence, principally in the form of imitative suicides and acts of aggression.

Video games are clearly capable of producing an increase in aggression and violence in the short term, although no long-term longitudinal studies capable of demonstrating long-term effects have been conducted. The relationship between media violence and real-world violence and aggression is moderated by the nature of the media content and characteristics of and social influences on the individual exposed to that content. Still, the average overall size of the effect is large enough to place it in the category of known threats to public health.

> *"There is no such thing as media vio-
> lence—at least not in the ways that we
> are used to talking about it."*

The Problem of Media Violence Is Exaggerated

Henry Jenkins

*In the following viewpoint, Henry Jenkins, a professor of litera-
ture and director of the Comparative Media Studies program at
the Massachusetts Institute of Technology, argues that the current cultural discussion concerning the effects of media violence
on society implies that media violence is a quantifiable phenomenon that can somehow be separated from art, literature, media,
and other social narratives. Jenkins states that violence is an in-
herent part of society and its cultural artifacts (such as movies,
books, and music) because aggression is a fundamental human
experience. Instead of banning violent works, Jenkins advocates
for broader and deeper discussions about media-constructed violence so that people can draw meaning from these depictions instead of simply feeling fearful of them—or worse, having no feeling about them at all.*

As you read, consider the following questions:

1. Why is Jenkins not surprised that the American Academy of Pediatrics reported that 100 percent of feature length cartoons released in America between 1937 and 1999 contained violent images?

2. Why are action stars often the most popular performers in the global market, according to Jenkins?

3. In Jenkins' opinion, what is "the problem" if, as he asserts, "the problem is not media violence per se"?

The news of last week's [April 2007] tragic shooting at Virginia Tech has brought the usual range of media reformers and culture warriors (never camera shy) scurrying back into the public eye to make their case that "media violence" must be contained, if not censored, if we are to prevent such bloodshed from occurring again. Almost immediately, longtime video game opponents Jack Thompson [an attorney and outspoken supporter of staunch government regulation of violence in the media] and Dr. Phil McGraw [psychologist and host of the TV show *Dr. Phil*] started appearing on television talk shows, predicting that the shooter [an English major named Seung-Hui Cho] would turn out to be a hardcore video game player. (The odds are certainly with them since a study released several years ago of frosh at 20 American colleges and universities found that a hundred percent of them had played games before going off to college and that on average college students spend more time each week playing games than reading recreationally, watching television, or going to the movies.) In fact, when the police searched the killer's dorm room, they found not a single game nor any signs of a game system.

The focus then quickly shifted with the news arguing first that the shooter was a heavy viewer of television "including television wrestling" and then linking some of the photographs he sent to NBC with images from Asian cult cinema—

most notably with the Korean film, *Oldboy*. An op-ed piece in the *Washington Post* asserted that *Oldboy* "must feature prominently in the discussion" of Mr. Cho's possible motivations, "even if no one has yet confirmed that Cho saw it" and then later, claims that Cho "was shooting a John Woo [director of often violent action films] movie in his head" as he entered the engineering building.

And then, of course, there was that damning evidence that he had constructed violent and aggressive fantasies during his creative writing classes. *Time* magazine even pathologizes the fact that he was a college student who didn't have a Facebook page! Talk about damned if you do and damned if you don't!

A Predictable Reaction

None of this should surprise us given the cycle of media coverage that has surrounded previous instances of school shootings. An initial period of shock is quickly followed by an effort to round up the usual suspects and hold them accountable—this is part of the classic psychology of a moral panic. In an era of 24-hour news, the networks already have experts on media violence in their speed dial, ready for them to arrive on the scene and make the same old arguments. As a media scholar, I find these comments predictable but disappointing: disappointing because they block us from having a deeper conversation about the place of violence in American culture.

I want to outline here another set of perspectives on the issue of media violence, ones that are grounded not in the literature of media effects but rather in the literature of cultural studies. I have plenty of criticisms of the media effects approach, which I outlined in my recent book, *Fans, Bloggers, and Gamers: Exploring Participatory Culture*, but for the most part, my focus here is more on what cultural studies might tell us about media violence than it is in critiquing that body of "research."

No Such Thing as Media Violence

So, let me start with an intentionally provocative statement. There is no such thing as media violence—at least not in the ways that we are used to talking about it—as something which can be easily identified, counted, and studied in the laboratory. Media violence is not something that exists outside of a specific cultural and social context. It is not one thing which we can simply eliminate from art and popular culture. It's not a problem we can make go away. Our culture tells lots of different stories about violence for lots of different reasons for lots of different audiences in lots of different contexts. We need to stop talking about media violence in the abstract and start talking about it in much more particularized terms.

Otherwise, we end up looking pretty silly. So, for example, a study endorsed by the American Academy of Pediatrics reported that 100 percent of feature length cartoons released in America between 1937 and 1999 contained images of violence. Here, we see the tendency to quantify media violence taken to its logical extreme. For this statement to be true, violence has to be defined here so broadly that it would include everything from the poison apple in *Snow White* to the hunter who shoots Bambi's mother, from Captain Hook's hook to the cobra that threatens to crush Mowgli in *The Jungle Book*, and that's just to stick with the Disney canon. The definition must include not only physical violence but threats of violence, implied violence, and psychological/emotional violence. Indeed, if we start from a definition that broad, we would need to eliminate conflict from our drama altogether in order to shut down the flow of media violence into our culture. Perhaps this is reason enough not to put pediatricians in charge of our national cultural policy anytime soon. Certainly few of us would imagine our culture improved if these films were stripped of their "violent" content or barred from exhibition.

Almost no one operates on a definition of violence that broad. Most of us make value judgments about the kinds of violence that worry us, judgments based on the meanings attached to the violence in specific representations, so church groups don't think twice about sending young kids to watch Jesus get beaten in *The Passion of the Christ*, and games reformers go after first-person shooters but not World War II simulation games (which coat their violence in patriotism and historical authenticity) even though this genre is now consistently outselling more antisocial titles in the video game marketplace.

Historical Pervasiveness of Media Violence

Why is violence so persistent in our popular culture? Because violence has been persistent as a theme across storytelling media of all kinds. A thorough account of violence in media would include: fairy tales such as "Hansel and Gretel," oral epics such as Homer's *The Iliad*, the staged violence of Shakespeare's plays, fine art paintings of the *Rape of the Sabine Women*, and stain glass window representations of Saints being crucified or pumped full of arrows, or for that matter, talk show conversations about the causes of school shootings. If we were to start going after media violence, then, we would need to throw out much of the literary canon and close down all of our art museums. Violence is fundamental to these various media because aggression and conflict is a core aspect of human experience. We need our art to help us make sense of the senselessness of violence in the real world, to provide some moral order, to help us sort through our feelings, to provoke us to move beyond easy answers and ask hard questions.

Again, nobody really means that we should get rid of all media violence, even if that's what they say often enough: we are all drawing lines and making distinctions, but all of those distinctions fly out the window when we read statistics that count the number of incidents of violence in an hour of television or when we read research that tells us how subjecting human lab rats to media violence may make them more or less aggressive.

In practice, it is hard to sustain the case that our culture is becoming more violent—not when we read it within the broader sweep of human history. Take a look at Robert Darnton's *The Great Cat Massacre*, which describes how workers in early modern Europe got their kicks by setting cats on fire and running them through the streets. Consider the role of public hangings in 19th century America. Or think about the popularity of cock fights and bear baiting in Shakespeare's London. We have, for the most part, moved from an era where humans sought entertainment through actual violence and into a period when we are amused through symbolic violence. Indeed, where people confront real violence on a regular basis, parents are often heartened to see their children playing violent video games—if for no other reason than they keep them off the streets and out of harm's way. (This is borne out by studies done in American ghettos or along the West Bank [middle East territory inhabited mostly by Palestinians, but occupied by Israeli military forces, leading to frequent violence].)

A Global Perspective

Nor can we argue that America is unique in its fascination with violent entertainment. I recently took a trip to Singapore and visited Haw Paw Villa, a cherished institution, where tourists can go into the mouth of hell and see grisly images of doomed souls being ground up, decapitated and dismembered, and impaled, drenched with buckets of red paint. For generations, Singaporeans have taken their children to this attraction for moral instruction, showing their young and impressionable ones what befalls those who lie to their parents or cheat on their examinations.

Our current framing of media violence assumes that it most often attracts us, that it inspires imitation, whereas throughout much of human history, representations of violence were seen as morally instructive, as making it less likely we are going to transgress various social prohibitions. When we read the lives of Saints, for example, we are invited to identify with the one suffering the violence and not the one committing it.

Media violence is not a uniquely American trend, though school shootings, by and large, are. Media violence is a global phenomenon. Indeed, the process of globalization is arguably increasing the vividness with which violence is represented not only in American media but in every major media-producing country. The physicality of violent representations is easily conveyed visually, allowing it to be understood and appreciated by people who might miss the nuances of spoken dialogue, who might not understand the language in which the film was produced or be able to read the subtitles. For that reason, action stars are often the most popular performers in the global market. As the United States, Japan, China, India, Korea, and a host of other film-producing countries compete for dominance in the global market place, we are seeing an escalation in the intensity of representations of violence. And American media often seems mild when compared with the kinds of things that can be found on screens in Asia or Latin America.

Part of the problem with the initial response to the news of the Virginia Tech shootings was the assumption that the young man involved would turn out to be a fan of American media violence. In fact, the evidence so far suggests that he was much more interested in Asian cinema, which should hardly be a surprise given that he came to the United States from Korea. Indeed, the news media has more recently noted similarities between his two-handed shooting techniques and the style made famous by Hong Kong action director John

Woo; they have also identified one of the images—where he waves a hammer—with a publicity still for the Korean film, *Oldboy*.

The Message of Violent Media

A news story in the *New York Times* describes *Oldboy* as an obscure cult film which appeals primarily to those who are interested in excessive violence. In fact, *Oldboy* has emerged as one of the most important films in the recent Korean film revival, one which has won awards from film festivals and has been playing in art houses across the country. While the film includes some of the most disturbing violence I've seen on screen in some time, that's precisely the point: the violence is meant to be disturbing. We watch the main character's slow descent into his own personal hell and then as he seeks to right wrongs that have been committed against him, we see him pushed into more and more violence himself. The filmmaker doesn't glorify the violence: he's horrified by it; he's using it to push past our own reserves and to get us to engage in issues of oppression and social aggression from a fresh perspective. I have always been struck by the fact that moral reformers rarely take aim at mundane and banal representations of violence though formulaic violence is pervasive in our culture. Almost always, they go after works that are acclaimed elsewhere as art—the works of [filmmaker] Martin Scorsese or [filmmaker] Quentin Tarantino, say—precisely because these works manage to get under their skin. For some of us, this provocation gets us thinking more deeply about the moral consequences of violence whereas others condemn the works themselves, unable to process the idea that a work might provoke us to reflect about the violence that it represents.

There's a kind of deadening literal mindedness about such criticisms: to represent something is to advocate it and to advocate it is to cause it. To watch this film and decide to imitate the protagonist is a misreading on the order of reading

The Need for Media Literacy

From the early days of radio and movies to the vast resources of today's World Wide Web, the mass media have been an object of fascination for youth. Yet parents, educators, and youth advocates have long been uneasy about many of the media messages that children and teenagers encounter. Popular culture can glamorize violence, irresponsible sex, junk food, drugs, and alcohol; it can reinforce stereotypes about race, gender, sexual orientation, and class; it can prescribe the lifestyle to which one should aspire, and the products one must buy to attain it.

Thus, it isn't surprising that calls to censor the mass media in the interest of protecting youth have been a mainstay of American politics for many years. . . .

Here is where media literacy education comes in. It not only teaches students how media messages are made and how they differ from reality, but it shows them how to analyze those messages, whether they involve commercial advertising, ethnic and gender stereotypes, violence, sexual decision-making, or other complex issues. As a White House report recently noted, media literacy empowers young people, not only to understand and evaluate the ideas found in popular culture, but "to be positive contributors to society, to challenge cynicism and apathy and to serve as agents of social change." Whatever the effectiveness of censorship, it can't accomplish this. Education in media literacy is thus not simply an alternative to censorship; it is far preferable to censorship, for it enhances rather than curtails young people's intellectual growth and their development into critically thinking adults.

Marjorie Heins and Christina Cho, Media Literacy:
An Alternative to Censorship, 2003.

Frankenstein and deciding to construct a creature from the parts of dead bodies or watching *A Clockwork Orange* and deciding it is fun to rape and terrorize senior citizens. It is certainly possible for someone who already is mentally disturbed to read these images out of context and ascribe to them meanings which are not part of the original, but then again, that's part of the point.

Reaffirmations of Individuals' Beliefs

If we take most of the existing research on media effects at face value, almost nothing would suggest that consuming media violence would turn an otherwise normal kid into a psychokiller. In practice, the research implies that consuming media violence can be one risk factor among many, that most incidents of real-world violence cannot be traced back to a single cause, and that real-world experiences (mental illness, drug abuse, histories of domestic violence, exposure to gangs, etc.) represent a much more immediate cause of most violent crime. Some research has shown that people in jail for violent crimes, in fact, consume less media violence than the general population, in part because they have not been able to afford consistent access to media technologies.

Understanding media violence as a risk factor—rather than as the cause of real-world violence—is consistent with some of the other things we know or think we know about media's influence. At the risk of reducing this to a simple formula, media is most powerful when it reaffirms our existing beliefs and behaviors, least powerful when it seeks to change them. We tend to read media representations against our perceptions of the real world and discard them if they deviate too dramatically from what we believe to be true.

In fact, children at a pretty young age—certainly by the time they reach elementary school—are capable of making at least crude distinctions between more or less realistic representations of violence. They can be fooled by media which offer ambiguous cues but they generally read media that seem realistic very differently than media that seem cartoonish or larger than life. For that reason, they are often much more emotionally disturbed by documentaries that depict predators and prey, war, or crime, than they are by the kinds of hyperbolic representations we most often are talking about when we refer to media violence.

Toward a New Conception of Media Violence

None of this is to suggest that the media we consume have no effect. Clearly, those kids who already live in a culture of violence are often drawn most insistently to violent entertainment. They may seek to use it to release their pent up anger and frustration; they may use its images to try to make sense of what they see as aggression and injustice around them; they may draw on its iconography to give some shape to their own inchoate feelings, and that's part of the way I would understand those disturbing photographs of Cho Seung-Hui striking poses from Asian action movies. We can't argue that these films had nothing to do with the horrors he committed on teachers and students at Virginia Tech. I think it does matter that he had access to some images of violence and not others and that he read those representations of violence through a set of emotional and psychological filters which distorted and amplified their messages.

Where does this leave us? It is meaningless as I have suggested to talk about regulating "media violence," as if all representations of violence were harmful. We need to get beyond rhetoric that treats media violence as a carcinogen, a poison or a pollutant. Rather, we should be asking ourselves what kinds of stories our culture tells about violence and how we are making sense of those representations in the context of our everyday lives. The problem is not media violence per se. If there is a problem, it is that so many of our contemporary works banalize violence through reliance on simple-minded formulas. What we need is more meaningful violence—representations of violence which incite and provoke us to think more deeply about the nature of aggression, trauma, and loss, representations which get under our skin and make it hard for us to simply sit back and relax in front of the screen. And we need to be having intelligent conversations about these media constructions of violence rather than trying to push such works away from us.

"Scientific research has repeatedly demonstrated that children learn what video games teach, and often that lesson is doing violence."

Video Games Foster Violent Behavior

David S. Bickham

In the following viewpoint, David S. Bickham, staff scientist at the Center on Media and Child Health and Children's Hospital in Boston, contends that violent video games can lead to violent behaviors in children. According to Bickham, violent video games typically reward aggression and teach players that violence is an acceptable form of problem solving. After long-term exposure to violent games, this message is ingrained in players and can lead to lasting negative effects, Bickham maintains.

As you read, consider the following questions:

1. According to Bickham, what specific characteristics of video games make them especially effective at instilling beliefs and behaviors in children?

David S. Bickham, "Testimony before Senate Judiciary Committee Subcommittee on the Constitution, Civil Rights, and Property Rights," March 29, 2006. http://judiciary.senate.gov. Reproduced by permission of the author.

2. Why, in Bickham's assessment, did early video game research show minimal differences between exposure to violent and nonviolent video games?

3. What are the bystander effect and the appetite effect produced by violent media, according to Bickham?

Video games are a relatively new form of entertainment media. While the body of evidence on video game violence is growing, we must consider it within the broader field of research exploring portrayals of violence in television, film, and other forms of visual media. There are five decades of media violence research based on a sound theoretical and empirical understanding of learning, aggression, and social cognition. A core ongoing project of the Center on Media and Child Health is the consolidation of all existing research on media effects into one publicly available database. After 3 years of work, the database includes over 1,200 research reports published in peer-reviewed scientific journals investigating the effects of media violence. These studies show consensus in the state of the science that a strong and consistent relationship exists between viewing violent media and increased levels of anxiety, desensitization and aggressive thoughts and behaviors among young people. This body of research derives from a broad spectrum of academic fields, including psychology, communications, public health, and criminal justice, and it draws added strength from the vast array of methodologies utilized by the different disciplines.

The Undeniable Draw of Video Games

Taken alone, no study is perfect. Even the best study design can be criticized for the limitations of its method. Taken together, however, each study about media violence provides a piece of a single puzzle that all interlock to reveal one picture.

In this case, that picture is clear—using violent media contributes to children's violent behavior. A variety of complementary methodologies that have resulted in similar findings have been used to generate this overall conclusion. Scientists have exposed children to violent media in laboratories and found that they behave more aggressively than children who saw non-violent television or played non-violent games. Using survey studies, scientists have found that even after controlling for dozens of complex environmental and individual characteristics linked to aggression, watching violent television and playing violent video games still increases the likelihood that a child will be violent. Researchers have followed children over their entire lives and found that viewing violent television as a child is one of the best predictors of criminal violent behaviors as an adult.

While the large body of research on violent television and film provides a solid foundation for our understanding of the effects of violent video games, there are reasons to believe that the influences of violent video games are stronger than those of other forms of screen violence. All media teach—whether by design or by default. Video games are exceptional teaching tools, incorporating many techniques that promote learning. First, video games are interactive, allowing the player to be closely involved with the main character and to control that character's actions. Second, video games directly reward the child's success in performing the actions, with visual effects, points, and opportunities to take on new challenges. Third, video games typically require almost complete attention, necessitating constant eyes-on-screen and hand-eye coordination to succeed in the game. Finally, video games are designed to be incredibly engaging and "fun," often leading children to slip deeply into a "flow state" in which they may be at increased susceptibility to the messages of the game. Scientific research has repeatedly demonstrated that children learn what video games teach, and often that lesson is doing violence.

Practicing Violence

We [Craig Anderson, Douglas A. Gentile, and Katherine E. Buckley, authors of *Violent Video Game Effects on Children and Adolescents*] do think the violent video games are likely to have a bigger effect [on viewers than watching violent movies], mainly because of the active participation. You are practicing all the aspects of violence: decision-making and carrying it out. That is not the case in a television show or violent movie. You're not the one who decides to pull the trigger or tries to hurt someone; you're simply the observer. Practicing making a particular kind of decision makes you better at making that kind of decision, just like practicing your multiplication tables makes you better at multiplication.

Interview with Craig Anderson,
Executive Intelligence Review, *June 1, 2007.*

With More Sophisticated Technologies Comes Increasingly Violent Reactions

Because the technology and media form are newer, investigating the effects of violent video games is a younger field than television violence research. Early video game research was inconsistent. Studies performed in the 1980s were limited by electronic gaming technology; at the time violent and non-violent games were often very similar. One study, for example, compared the effects of playing *Missile Command* (considered the violent game) to *Pac-Man* (considered the non-violent game). Both games feature abstract geometric icons interacting with one another; both have the player's icons destroying or devouring other icons. As video games have become more graphically sophisticated and capable of depicting violence in a much more graphic and realistic way, the differences between violent and non-violent video games have dramatically increased. Not surprisingly, research exploring the effects of these newer games is much more clear and consistent than previous research. The newest research has definitively and repeatedly converged on the conclusion that playing violent video games is linked to children's aggression.

We all know that children are not automatons who mimic everything they see; their behavior is much more complicated than that. However, there is a widely held misconception that unless children immediately imitate the violence they experience in a video game, they are unaffected by it. Children who play *Grand Theft Auto* don't immediately begin stealing cars and shooting police officers. As a result, many would have you believe that this means that violent video games have no influence. We cannot assume that the absence of immediate and direct imitation means that there are no effects on children.

In rare situations violence from media may be directly imitated after a single exposure, but the most pervasive effects of violent media are not direct imitation and come from repeated viewings. With each exposure, the child's perception of the world is shifted to include violence as a common and acceptable occurrence. The child's behaviors evolve to correspond with this perception and can follow "behavioral scripts" established through experiencing violent media.

Positive Reinforcement for Violent Behavior

Four primary effects of violent media that have been consistently documented in the scientific literature: the aggressor, victim, bystander, and appetite effects. The aggressor effect is the most well known—using violent media increases the likelihood that a child will think and behave aggressively toward others. The victim effect is the tendency for users of violent media to see the world as a scary and violent place promoting anxiety and protective behaviors. The bystander effect describes how violent media desensitizes its users to the real-life violence making them generally less caring and sympathetic to victims of violence and less likely to intervene when they witness violence. Finally, the appetite effect demonstrates that using violent media often increases children's desire to see more violence.

While each of these effects can have substantial influence on children's behaviors, the aggressor effect is perhaps the most troublesome because it puts children at immediate risk of committing violence. It is, therefore, critical to understand how exposure to violent video games translates into aggressive behavior. This process is grounded in our understanding of how children learn, how aggression in general is cultivated, and how video game violence affects its users.

Violent video games present a world in which violence is justified, rewarded, and often the only option for success. Exposure to this world primes children for hostile thoughts and behaviors immediately after playing a game. When children play violent video games, they become both physically and mentally aroused. Their heart rates increase and their blood pressure rises. They begin to think aggressively and to solve problems with violence. In this heightened and primed state, children are more likely to perceive other people's behaviors as aggressive and they are more likely to respond aggressively. In laboratory studies designed to test this effect, participants who played violent video games were more likely to punish competitors than participants who played non-violent games.

Over time, repeated exposure to violent media can have long-term effects. A person's pattern of behavior can become more aggressive through the adoption of aggressive skills, beliefs, and attitudes, desensitization to violence, and an aggressive approach to interactions with other people. Scientific findings have repeatedly provided solid evidence for this process—using violent media as a child predicts aggressive behavior in adulthood.

A Varying but Always Violent Response

Violent video games often have subtle effects but may lead to dramatic consequences for some children. Certain characteristics make some children more susceptible to media effects, while other children are more resilient. However, no known factor or set of factors has yet been identified that completely safeguards children from the influences of violent media.

Children's susceptibility to the effects of media violence varies with their age. Children younger than eight years are more vulnerable to media violence effects because they have not yet developed the ability to discriminate fully between fantasy and reality in media content. Research has consistently shown that young children often behave more aggressively than older children do after playing violent video games.

Children who identify with the perpetrator of media violence are also at increased risk of becoming aggressive. Violent video games, particularly the aptly named "first-person shooter" games, place the player in the role of the violent perpetrator. This level of involvement is likely to increase the player's identification with the violence and its subsequent cognitive and behavioral effects.

Cognitive and emotional maturity tends to increase children's resistance to the effects of violent media. It is important to remember, however, that neither these nor any other set of characteristics fully protects a child from all of the subtle and pervasive effects of violent media.

> *"Of course, once the dust settles, it may really be that video games, like most other forms of entertainment, are simply that: entertainment, neither helpful nor harmful."*

Video Games Have Become a Scapegoat for Violent Behavior

Christopher J. Ferguson

Christopher J. Ferguson is an assistant professor of behavioral sciences and criminal justice at Texas A&M University. In the following viewpoint, he argues that it has become all too common to blame video games for inciting individuals to act out in a violent manner. Ferguson maintains that research has not shown a direct correlation between playing violent video games and perpetrating violence. However, he asserts that despite this lack of correlation, the media, politicians, and social scientists are willing to insist that a connection exists between video game violence and real-word violence to further their own agendas and avoid discussing sensitive issues, such as family violence, that may actually contribute to a more violent society.

As you read, consider the following questions:

1. What flaws did Ferguson find in his meta-analysis of twenty-five violent-game studies?

2. In the author's view, why does the "video-game hypothesis" remain so active despite contradictory evidence?

3. According to Ferguson, what is the video game *Re-Mission*, and how is it being used?

In the wake of the Virginia Tech shootings, it was distressing to see the paroxysms of neurotic finger-pointing and "expert witnessing" that inevitably followed. Beyond noting simply that a bad (evil, some would say) man chose one day to make the lives of other individuals as hellish as he felt his own to be, I don't think we'll ever come up with much more of a scientific explanation for what leads people, mostly men, to become mass murderers. Let me put that another way: Beyond individuals who actually threaten in advance to carry out school shootings (which a recent Secret Service report concluded was the only really useful indicator), no other behavior is particularly predictive of such acts of senseless violence.

That's not very satisfying, is it? Perhaps for that reason, it seems to me that increasingly, as a culture, we have shied away from holding people responsible for their behaviors, and instead prefer to seek out easy or even abstract entities to blame. Events like school shootings tend to make people nervous. Nervous people like reassurance. We would like to think that such events can be explained, predicted, and prevented. We like scientists and politicians who stand up and claim to have the answers so that we can fix the problem.

The New Media Violence Scapegoat

The difficulty is that this often leads to a witch hunt or moral panic, wherein explanations rely on weak social science or what is politically expedient. In past centuries, a variety of art forms have taken the blame for society's problems. From literature to religious texts, to jazz, rock 'n' roll, and rap, to television, movies, and comic books, people have viewed various media as being responsible for personal failings, as if such media were like the serpent in the Garden of Eden, leading us astray from our natural goodness. Increasingly, in the past two decades, video games have been the scapegoat du jour. The video-game platform is the newest kid on the media block and, as such, is subject to a particularly high dose of suspicion and scrutiny. I think that this is wrong and, indeed, dangerous.

It seemed that the Virginia Tech rampage was barely over before a few pundits began speculating on the role of video games. The lawyer and activist Jack Thompson asserted that violent games such as *Counter-Strike* may have been responsible for the shooter's actions. Although I have heard little to indicate conclusively that the perpetrator was an avid gamer, the prevalence of game playing among young men makes it likely that he would have crossed paths with a violent game at some point ("He played *Spy Versus Spy* once when he was 12, that's the culprit!"). For instance, a 1996 study found that 98.7 percent of children of either gender played some video games, with violent games, like *Streetfighter II*, particularly popular among young men (93 percent of whom had played that one game alone). Since most young men today play violent video games, it is usually not hard to "link" a violent crime with video-game playing if you are so inclined. This is the classic error of using a high-base-rate (very common) behavior to explain a low-base-rate (rare) behavior. Using video-game-playing habits to predict school shootings is about as useful as noting that most or all school shooters were in the habit of wearing sneakers and concluding that sneakers must be responsible for such violence.

The Lack of Evidence Relating Video Games and Violent Behavior

I actually do research on violent video games. I certainly don't speak for others in the field, some of whom I know will disagree with my perspective, but I do speak from a familiarity with the research and the literature. One meta-analysis of video-game studies, conducted this year by John Sherry, of Michigan State University, found little support for the belief that playing violent games causes aggression. Recently I completed my own meta-analytic review (published in the journal *Aggression and Violent Behavior*) of 25 violent-game studies and found that publication bias and the use of poor and unstandardized measures of aggression were significant problems for this area of research.

My meta-analysis concluded that there was no evidence to support either a causal or correlational relationship between video games and aggressive behavior. My impression is that social science made up its mind that video games cause aggression before many data were available, and has subsequently attempted to fit square pieces of evidence into round theoretical holes. The threshold for what appears to constitute "evidence" is remarkably low. Admittedly, publication bias (the tendency to publish articles that support a hypothesis and not publish those that don't) is very likely a widespread problem in the social sciences and is not unique to video-game studies. Perhaps this is really a reflection on human nature. I may sound hopelessly postmodern here, but sometimes we forget that scientists are mere humans, and that the process of science, as a human enterprise, may always have difficulty rising above a collective and dogmatic pat on the back rather than a meaningful search for truth.

Creating Studies to Support Policy Decisions

Unfortunately, I think it is a worrisome reflection on social science in general that social scientists may be too prone to

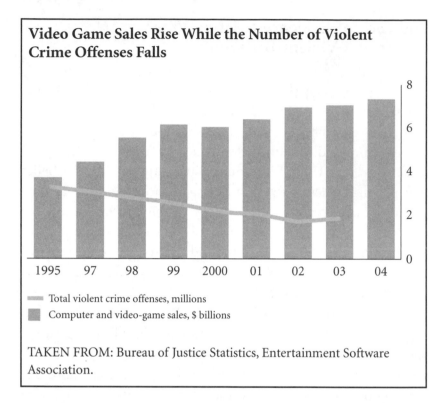

Video Game Sales Rise While the Number of Violent Crime Offenses Falls

Total violent crime offenses, millions

Computer and video-game sales, $ billions

TAKEN FROM: Bureau of Justice Statistics, Entertainment Software Association.

make big and frightening pronouncements from weak results. That violent crime rates in the United States have gone down significantly since 1994 (despite some small recent increases) while video games have gotten more popular and more violent should, in and of itself, be sufficient to reject the video-game-violence hypothesis (and the rest of the media-violence hypothesis with it). Some media researchers attempt to defuse this argument by suggesting that "other factors" are at play, but no theory should be allowed to survive such a retreat to an unfalsifiable position—that it never need actually fit with real-world data. Could you imagine how far the debate on global warming would have gotten if the earth's atmospheric temperatures were decreasing while pollutants were being released?

In my opinion, the video-game hypothesis remains because it fits well with the dogma of social science (which has yet to escape from an obsession with deterministic learning models that view humans as passive programmed machines rather than active in determining their own behavior), and it is politically expedient. Politicians can use "media violence" to enact popular (but unconstitutional) legislation censoring or otherwise limiting access to violent media, legislation that can appeal to both political conservatives and political liberals. (Religious conservatives might be bemused to know that some media-violence researchers recently published an article suggesting that reading passages from the Bible with violent content increases "aggression" in much the same way that video games supposedly do. So if video games have to be restricted from children, apparently so do at least some portions of the Bible.) By stating that such legislation is based on "concern for children," politicians can cast their opponents as being unconcerned with children while stripping parents of their rights to decide what media are appropriate for their children. In such a political environment, the video-game-violence hypothesis has persisted long after it should have been laid to rest.

Blaming Video Games, Ignoring Human Nature

All this is no idle concern. Media issues serve to distract us from more-sensitive topics that may be real contributors to violent behavior, notably violence in families—although in fairness, not all abused people become violent offenders. I also posit that many of us prefer to blame others, particularly an abstract entity such as the media, for our problems rather than accept personal responsibility when we or our children behave badly. That's the crux of it, I think. Video games, like the rest of the media, form a faceless specter that we have called into being with our own internal desires for sex and violence, yet can turn against when we need a straw man to blame for our own recklessness.

What's lost in the discussion is that there have been several publications suggesting that violent games may be related to increased performance in some areas of cognition, particularly visuospatial cognition. This is a new research area, and I certainly don't wish to reverse the error of overstating the link between video games and aggression by producing my own overstatement. But I do think that, instead of fueling up the bonfires and throwing in the game consoles, we need to have a serious discussion of both sets of potential effects. Given the allure of violent video games, it may be advisable to consider how some games with violent content may be used to further educational purposes. For instance, a first-person-shooter game (though certainly a mild one compared with some) called *Re-Mission* is being studied in relation to young adults with cancer. One group of youths who played this game demonstrated better cancer-treatment adherence, better self-efficacy and quality of life, and more cancer-related knowledge than did those in a control group who did not play the game. Of course, once the dust settles, it may really be that video games, like most other forms of entertainment, are simply that: entertainment, neither helpful nor harmful.

I don't know how it came to be that we, as a culture, ceased holding people responsible for their actions. How did we come to feel that we are programmed like machines? How did we come to embrace the Brave New World not as a dystopia to be feared but as a panacea for all of our human guilt? When a man or woman picks up a weapon and premeditates the end of another human life, it is not because he or she was programmed by a video game but because that individual made a conscious choice—not to play a game, but to kill. This darkness lurks not within our computers, televisions, books, or music, but rather within our species and, sometimes, ourselves.

| "Games are . . . complex problem-solving systems that develop logical thinking, decision making, and encourage a scientific approach to the unknown."

Video Games Are Useful Educational Tools

Lee Wilson

Lee Wilson argues in the following viewpoint that not all video games are rife with violence; instead, many games challenge players to utilize high-order thinking and problem-solving skills. According to Wilson, several popular games focus on history, economics, mathematics, and other subjects that make them useful additions to classroom education. Wilson, a veteran in the education business, owns the consulting firm Headway Strategies, which provides advice for companies seeking to market products for the K–12 education sector.

As you read, consider the following questions:

1. How do games like *Railroad Tycoon* and *Muzzy Lane's Making History* work as effective teaching tools, and what skills must students utilize when playing them, according to Wilson?

Lee Wilson, "Getting It Wrong: Slaying Myths about Video Games," *Technology and Learning*, September 15, 2007. Copyright © 2007 NewBay Media, LLC. Reproduced by permission.

2. In Wilson's view, why do games such as *Grand Theft Auto* and *Postal* create such a negative public view of video games?

3. What topics are explored in games developed by the Serious Games initiative?

Two years ago I began to play *World of Warcraft* (WoW) as a way to stay in touch with my teenage sons while I was on the road.

WoW is the market leader of a new generation of computer games characterized as "massively multiplayer"—more than 9 million people around the globe play Blizzard Entertainment's WoW together on the Internet. In the evenings my sons and I would meet online, playing and chatting about our day and the things we were doing in the game.

After a few weeks something about the underlying structure of the game began to look very familiar. When you look past the Orcs, Gnomes, and other fanciful inhabitants and elements, you find Blizzard has built an elegant and engaging learning management system. WoW does an outstanding job of guiding players to their zone of proximal development and provides a never-ending stream of feedback and fresh challenges while leaving the player in charge. My guess is that philosopher and psychologist Jean Piaget would be proud and amused to see his ideas implemented in this context and on such a global scale.

A Potential Teaching Tool

Slowly I began to unlearn everything I thought I knew about video games. I read *New York Times* science writer Steven Johnson's 2005 book *Everything Bad Is Good for You*, where he makes the compelling case that the hefty cognitive load of engaging in popular culture is steadily expanding our intellectual capacity. Video games, cultural phenomena since the late '70s, are a big part of this trend. The first thing any video game has to do is teach the player how to use it. Games that fail at this challenge fail in the market for the simple reason that players just abandon them. As a result, video game developers have become adept practitioners of some of the best findings of cognitive neuroscience. Games are also complex problem-solving systems that develop logical thinking, decision making, and encourage a scientific approach to the unknown.

I have since discovered a very vibrant community of academics, educators, students, and business types who agree that video games have a powerful potential for learning and training. As well, there is a growing body of practice, products, and research to support the notion that games are a valuable addition to the set of tools teachers are using in formal education.

Preconceived Negative Attitudes Toward Video Games

But real barriers abound. Among them are the general unfamiliarity of educators with the modern gaming world, the inability of games to fit neatly into the traditional class time frame, and the lack of evaluation tools to measure what is being learned. Many of these are being addressed with innovative and flexible solutions. However, many additional perceived barriers to integrating video games into learning are ill-founded. In fact, there are a number of well-circulated myths that have reinforced widespread negative attitudes toward games. Following, we address those myths.

Myth #1—Games Are All About Twitch Speed, Not Higher Order Thinking Skills

When most people think about video games for learning they think of titles from the mid-'90s that were basically animated flash cards. *Math Blaster*, *Mavis Beacon*, and most of what is sold as "edutainment" fit this profile. These games are fairly rigid, linear, and reward answering a question quickly rather than thinking through complex problems.

By contrast the best of today's games put players into complex simulations they can freely explore. Educators have always used simulations to help students connect content to real-world examples—to wit, the "a train leaves New York going 45 mph and another leaves Buffalo going 35 mph. . ." math simulation.

What video games allow are much richer simulations that can form the basis of deep classroom discussions spanning multiple subject areas. Players are challenged to tackle deeply nested problems, and there are multiple paths to success. Meanwhile, they're attuning themselves to the game's culture, the human social context.

Utilizing Multiple Academic Skills

In one of the many scenarios in *Railroad Tycoon* (Firaxis Games), players have to find the most efficient railroad route between New York and Buffalo. It turns out that running your trains up the Hudson River Valley rather than the much more direct route through the mountains is the most efficient way despite a much longer track. In addition to this challenge, players have to build stations in the most profitable spots, buy locomotives balancing speed against cost, encourage economic development to generate rail traffic, and run their railroad profitably. History, science, economics, and geography all come into play.

Muzzy Lane's Making History is another excellent example. This game simulates Europe just before World War II. Teams of students are assigned to lead individual countries, and as they take turns the game uses a combination of real economic and military data, historical events, and the choices of the teams to allow the students to "play" history. Teachers have reported finding groups of students in the lunchroom arguing about the Potsdam Conference. They have also observed emergent forms of leadership as students initiate informal diplomatic negotiations around the classroom. This game draws on

Boys Able to Distinguish Between Video Game and Real-World Behavior

The boys we spoke with were articulate about their attitudes and behavior regarding video games. Boys from a range of racial/ethnic and socioeconomic backgrounds used games in similar ways and raised similar themes. Boys use violent games specifically (a) as a means to express fantasies of power and glory, (b) to explore and master what they perceived as exciting and realistic environments, and (c) as a tool to work out their feelings of anger and stress. Games—especially violent or sports games—are also social tools that allow boys to compete with and/or work cooperatively with peers. Boys gain status among peers by owning or mastering these popular games. This supports the idea that video game play with violent content may serve a function similar to rough-and-tumble play for young adolescent boys.

Most boys did not believe that they were negatively influenced by violent games. All boys believed that they knew the difference between behaviors that are rewarded in games and behaviors in real life. They clearly distinguished between antisocial or violent behaviors that were unlikely to occur in their lives (e.g., using powerful weapons and stealing cars) and those that were likely to occur (e.g., swearing and intimidation). In distinguishing between real life and the game world, they focused on actions rather than realism of graphic depictions.

Cheryl K. Olson, Lawrence A. Kutner, and Dorothy E. Warner,
Journal of Adolescent Research, *January 2008.*

the core academic disciplines of reading, math, and social studies while also encouraging teamwork, initiative, creativity, problem solving, and leadership.

In the examples given above there is no right answer, only multiple paths to success, and there is as much to be learned from failure as from success. Most important, the games encourage students to use core academic skills in the pursuit of solving complex problems. Thinking deeply, not flicking buttons, is key.

Myth #2—Games Are Just About Violence and Sex

Some notorious games like *Grand Theft Auto* (Rockstar Games) and *Postal* (Running with Scissors) have drawn press and political attention for extreme violence and sexual situations. Given the level of coverage these titles have earned it is easy for those who are not exposed to the much larger gaming world to assume that all games are like this.

In fact, there have always been lots of video games that don't fit this profile. Venerable titles like *SimCity* (Maxis), which allows users to build and manage a metropolis, and *Civilization* (Firaxis Games), where players guide a civilization from its founding to the space age, have been used in classrooms for years. The Learning Company's *Oregon Trail* pioneered this market, allowing students to retrace the steps of history and to bring to life the challenges and decisions that settlers faced.

Developing Games that Focus on Important Issues

The Serious Games initiative, spearheaded by Ben Sawyer, is a consortium of developers and academics that is building games for educational, social, military, medical, and corporate environments. Recent titles have tackled subjects like Mid-East negotiations (*Peacemaker*), refugees (United Nations World Food Programme's *Food Force*), global warming (*CO2FX*), mental calisthenics (Nintendo's *Big Brain Academy*), gerrymandering (*The ReDistricting Game*), and environmental studies (*Quest Atlantis*). The military has successfully used games to simulate the cultural negotiation needed in Iraq to give soldiers an opportunity to practice before going overseas.

In *Quest Atlantis*, players focus on environmental issues as they assume the role of a field researcher helping a community wrestling with declining water quality. As they explore the world, they interview loggers, environmentalists, municipal workers, and native tribes. They also take measurements and use the scientific method to understand what they are seeing. Students make recommendations for how to deal with the problems that balance science, social equity, and economics.

Educational Games Can Be Visually Stimulating

A related concern is the perception that any game used in the classroom has to compete with the slick production values of commercial games. This too turns out to be false. A good example is *The ReDistricting Game* from USC's Annenberg Center, which challenges players to draw up new congressional districts. This simple, Web-based game (anyone with a browser can play) puts the player in the hot seat to meet a range of conflicting goals by juggling demographic data, legal requirements, and political demands. You have to satisfy members of your own party while also satisfying a judge's legal review, incumbents of both parties, and citizen feedback. In the process you use math to make sure districts are relatively even in population but drastically different in party affiliation. Players also gain an understanding of our political party system and the ability to work with interactive cartography (the game interface is a map). *ReDistricting* makes gerrymandering a visceral experience rather than an abstract concept batted around on the editorial page.

> *"For 50 years and upwards, the movies have been assiduously removing the moral context from the images of violence they deal in."*

The Lack of Moral Context in Movies Is Harmful

James Bowman

In the following viewpoint, James Bowman argues that violence in the movies has become "contextless," as heroes and antiheroes perform violence for selfish motives and without recourse to any higher purpose. Bowman contends that a hero's violent acts are often shown as justified because the hero has usually been wronged or abused—and the violent retaliation is a form of revenge. This justification often touches viewers who, dealing with their own feelings of self-pity, often desire to strike back for the perceived wrongs done to them. Bowman worries, however, that some people—validated by these film interpretations—do lash out and cause real tragedies. Bowman serves as a resident scholar for the Ethics and Public Policy Center. He has been a movie and media critic for numerous publications since the 1990s and has authored the book Honor: A History.

As you read, consider the following questions:

1. Bowman concedes that the individual who killed thirty-two people at Virginia Tech University in April 2007 probably did not learn his violent techniques from the movie *Oldboy;* what instead does the author argue the killer took from the movie?

2. What violence-related trend does Bowman say began with or was at least continued by the movie *Yojimbo?*

3. Why does the author argue that violence itself cannot be the problem in modern media?

Too bad Jack Valenti [former president of the Motion Picture Association of America (MPAA), and creator of the MPAA rating system] was taken from us so soon after the massacre at Virginia Tech on April 16th [2007] had rekindled the debate over violence in the movies. His defense of the ratings system he devised back in the 1960s to take the place of the old Hays Code—now regarded, absurdly, as a form of censorship—might have served as a timely reminder of the extent to which that system was a product of its time and place. The liberationist mentality, still strongly characteristic of so many of those who, like me, came of age then, depended on a severing of the ties between individual behavior and its social consequences that had always, up until then, been taken for granted. This led to a similar dissociation between art and its effects on its audience, on the one hand, and the realities it represents on the other.

The Rise of the Individual

The reality principle has thus been banished from film as from the other arts. Utopianism, with its usual genius for reversing the meanings of words—compare "people's democracies"—has ensured that when, today, someone says "in reality" what he means is "this is what *I* think." Older readers may remember that it used to mean "what we can agree is the case, independently of any individual's opinion." Now there is no such agreement. Individual opinion is king. We are all reality entrepreneurs, manufacturing and producing private realities that we then attempt to market to others. One of many unfortunate consequences is that "It's just a movie" has become the battle cry—at once smug and despairing—of those who believe passionately that the abolition of reality was not too high a price to pay for the utopian dream of making each man absolute monarch of the fantasy kingdom inside his own head.

It is all a lie, of course, as utopianism always is—and as episodes like the shootings at Virginia Tech occasionally remind us. Or ought to remind us. So powerful is the liberationist myth, however, that the media echo chamber was swiftly filled with the sound of fantasy's champions sharpening their swords for the satisfying work of hacking to pieces one or another of the straw men they always construct for themselves on these occasions. Here's a fair sampling from Sam Leith of the London *Daily Telegraph*:

> The notion persists that there is a monkey-see, monkey-do relationship between violent or pornographic art and violent behavior by its consumers, who—we're told—are "desensitized" by it. This works both ways, incidentally. Censorship junkies believe art shapes societies in a simple way; as do totalitarians. The result—in Soviet Russia and Nazi Germany—was bad art rather than good citizens.

Speaking as a "censorship junkie," I repudiate, along with the scare quotes around "desensitized," both totalitarian ambitions and the belief that art shapes societies in a simple way. Art shapes societies in many ways, none of them simple—though they are no less obvious for that.

A Culture of Self-Pity

In *Oldboy*, for example, the Korean film that has been most often cited as having influenced the Virginia Tech shooter, there is not all that much violence, and very little of what there is involves gunplay. In the two most gruesome scenes, when a man pulls teeth with a claw hammer or, later, cuts off his own tongue with a pair of scissors, the camera cuts away after giving us only a taste of the gore. Neither "violence" nor its techniques is what the murderer could conceivably have learned from this movie. But neither can it be merely coincidental that it is an appeal to, and is itself positively drenched in, self-pity—which seems much more likely to have been instrumental in motivating a morose loner with a grudge against the world and a conceit of himself as some kind of artist to turn his violent fantasies into reality.

The pervasive self-pity of adolescent culture, and its flirtation with suicide, goes way beyond Mr. Leith's "monkey-see, monkey-do relationship," but it is no less influential for that. And it is only one of several aspects of that culture which, if there were any prosecutor in Virginia bold enough to put them in the dock, would have to plead *nolo contendere* [no contest]. The other film that some have specified as a likely influence on the killer was John Woo's *Face/Off* (1997), which may or may not have taught him how cool two-fisted gunplay looks—as was suggested in the *Washington Post* by Stephen Hunter whose own novel, *Point of Impact*, had just been filmed as *Shooter*. But there can scarcely be a doubt that *Face/Off* is the *reductio ad absurdum* [reduction to the absurd] of the moral-equivalence theory of violence that has reigned supreme in Hollywood since [actor] Clint Eastwood first took his six-shooter to Italy. Can't anyone identify this demoralization of violence, not in one film but in hundreds of them, as one of the killer's accomplices?

Villains as Heroes

If you go back today to re-view *A Fistful of Dollars* (1964), you are likely to be amazed at how little blood there is. Though the body count is unusually high, every time someone is shot he simply clutches his chest and falls over. The wound is almost never shown. This style was left over from the old-fashioned, moralistic Western that was interested in the rights and wrongs of violence, and had not yet discovered the purely aesthetic appeal of violent death. The only hint of what was so soon to come was the "graphic" scene in which Mr. Eastwood gets caught and is savagely beaten up by the bad guys. Of course, he's a bad guy too. They're all bad guys. That was the point, as it also had been in [Japanese film director] Akira Kurosawa's original, *Yojimbo*, of 1961. Both Clint and Kurosawa's hero, played by Toshiro Mifune, were just less bad than the rest: high-minded killers who were capable, at a given moment and almost on impulse, of acts of humanity or compassion that cost them dearly.

In *Yojimbo*, Mifune was also beaten up and thus started a trend—or continued one that was lifted from Hollywood *noir* pictures like *The Glass Key* (1942) or *The Big Sleep* (1946)—of the hero as spectacular sufferer, appealing not to our admiration or moral approval but to our pity. This, too, is part of the debasement and demoralization of the culture—which is what produces moral monsters and not, by themselves, the images of graphic violence that have become so common since 1964. *Grindhouse* by [filmmaker] Quentin Tarantino, the high priest of fantastical and purely aesthetic violence, was released two weeks after *Shooter* and ten days before the Blacksburg rampage. It flopped, but the number one movie in the country the following weekend—and for weeks afterwards—was *Disturbia*, which features that Hollywood favorite, a serial killer (David Morse), who is so much taken for granted that the movie doesn't even bother to give him any motivation. The ordinary guy-next-door who just likes killing people has become as much an American movie cliché as the cowboy or the gangster used to be.

Discussions on Media Violence Emphasize the Effect on the Individual

Undergraduate students love to talk about violence in the media. Whenever the topic arises, I brace myself for the following discussion. This conversation begins when a student, usually male, announces that he grew up playing *Mortal Kombat* (or *Doom*, or *Grand Theft Auto*, or some other video game gore fest), and lo and behold, he did not grow up to be a violent person. Therefore, he announces with definitive authority, violence in the media does not matter. This assertion inevitably is contested by another student, usually female, who proclaims with equally definitive authority that violence in the media is a cataclysmic problem. She knows this because she babysits her 7-year-old nephew, and whenever he plays violent video games, he beats up his little sister. Without fail, someone invokes the C word—Columbine—and before I know it, my students are debating with passion whether violence in the media causes individuals to become violent. . . .

Naomi R. Rockler,
Popular Communication, *2006.*

The Problem with Contextless Violence

Mr. Leith's animadversion upon us "censorship junkies" handsomely allows that "the work of art is involved in the violence" but, he adds, "it does not, as some people seem to think, 'stand to reason' that the relationship is a simple one of causation. Rather, the evidence suggests (given the number of consumers of violent art who don't go on killing sprees) that the psychosis attaches itself to the artwork, rather than that the artwork causes the psychosis." Once again he disingenuously pretends to believe that causation can only be "simple" when we know it's not. What does "stand to reason" is that when suicide-chic is just one more lifestyle choice that the culture affords the morally and spiritually impoverished youths who have come hungry to its smorgasbord, or when they will have seen few or no examples of violence placed in the kind of moral context afforded by old-fashioned Westerns or other pre-ratings movies, there cannot be *no* connection between these facts and occasional outbursts of violence by certain of the more unstable sort of movie fans.

The problem is really with the concept of "violence" itself. Violence can't be the problem. Popular culture has always been full of violence. The problem is one of *contextless* violence. For 50 years and upwards, the movies have been assiduously removing the moral context from the images of violence they deal in. From the samurai epics of the great Kurosawa to the lowliest shoot 'em up the message is the same, and it is a message of moral equivalence. There are no good guys or bad guys but only those who suffer or those who inflict generic violence. Heroes may be *cool*, but this isn't at all the same thing as being good. Being good would be an embarrassment to the cool hero. Prowess in killing may still be admired, but that admiration is unlikely to extend to anyone who has a reason to kill beyond his own purposes of revenge, self-protection, or self-enrichment. This reduction of violence to a matter of aesthetics must be what appeals to sick, self-obsessed kids. For them as for us, it is not "just a movie" but rather another re-affirmation of the liberationist principle that all art is or can be self-justifying fantasy.

Periodical Bibliography

The following articles have been selected to supplement the diverse views presented in this chapter.

Lisa Brooten
"Media and Violence: Gendering the Debates," *Culture & Society*, July 2006.

Elizabeth K. Carll
"Violent Video Games: Rehearsing Aggression," *Chronicle of Higher Education*, July 13, 2007.

David Edelstein
"Now Playing at Your Local Multiplex: Torture Porn," *New York Magazine*, February 6, 2006.

Lis Else and Mike Holderness
"Are the Kids Alright After All?" *New Scientist*, July 2, 2005.

Daniel Koffler
"Grand Theft Scapegoat," *Reason*, October 2005.

Bowie Kotria
"Sex and Violence: Is Exposure to Media Content Harmful to Children?" *Children & Libraries: The Journal of the Association for Library Service to Children*, Summer-Fall 2007.

Chris Mercogliano
"An Amish Farmer's Insight," *Encounter*, Winter 2006.

Justin Peters
"Blood, Guts and Entertainment," *Reason*, February 2006.

Barbara Righton
"It's a Scene from *24*—No, It's a Car Ad," *Maclean's*, December 18, 2006.

Seth Schiesel
"Under Glare of Scrutiny, A Game Is Toned Down," *New York Times*, October 29, 2007.

A.O. Scott
"True Horror: When Movie Violence Is Random," *New York Times*, March 23, 2003.

USA Today
"Media Violence May Be Real Culprit Behind Virginia Tech Tragedy," April 19, 2007.

CHAPTER 2

How Should Media Violence Be Regulated?

Chapter Preface

In April 2007, the Federal Communications Commission (FCC) released a report to Congress on the state of television violence and its impact on young viewers. According to the FCC report, which took two years to compile, American families have deep concerns about the frequency and content of violent programming on television. The commission noted that technology aids—such as the V-chip implanted in nearly all television sets—have failed to gain wide acceptance or use in the public, and therefore some other measure should be utilized to help parents restrict the number of violent broadcasts that reach children. Agreeing with research that draws a correlation between exposure to television violence and childhood aggression, the FCC asserted that Congress has the power to limit violent programming because it can be deemed a matter of public interest—in the same way sexually explicit material and profanity have already been restricted.

Capitalizing on the FCC report, Senator Jay Rockefeller of West Virginia announced that he would introduce a bill in Congress to empower the FCC to restrict violent programming on cable, satellite, and broadcast television. The FCC report had suggested limiting violent programming to certain hours of the day (specifically, late at night when the number of young viewers declines) and compelling cable and satellite companies to offer subscribers only the channels they wanted, thus giving parents the ability to keep objectionable channels out of their programming packages. Rockefeller supported the à la carte programming option but made clear that many possibilities were under consideration. "I fear that graphic violent programming has become so pervasive and has been shown to be so harmful, we are left with no choice but to have the government step in," Rockefeller affirmed in June 2007.

By the end of Congress's August 2007 recess, the television violence bill had still not been introduced. Rockefeller's staff attributed the delay to poor timing, insisting that other high-priority bills were taking up the legislature's agenda. Critics, however, suggest that the bill stalled because of the lukewarm reception of the FCC report in Congress and in the media. Senator Frank Lautenberg of New Jersey maintained that the popularity of many violent television programs proves that Americans are not likely to endorse restrictive legislation. "We tried to regulate behavior before," Lautenberg said. "It was called Prohibition. It didn't work because the public appetite was not there." Lautenberg and other naysayers continue to argue that it would be an impossible task to decide what types of violence should be targeted given that a wide variety of programs—from cartoons to network news—contain violent images.

In the following chapter, critics and supporters of regulating media violence debate who should be entrusted with that power. Although most parents agree that there is too much violence on television, in video games and movies, and even within the lyrics of pop songs, there is no consensus that government action is needed to police the media. Most parents still attest that they should have the sole authority to oversee the types of media messages that enter their homes. Rockefeller and his supporters affirm that FCC regulation would give parents more control over their own policing powers, but so far the requisite legislation has not materialized.

> *"Just as the government has a compelling interest in protecting children from sexually explicit programming, a strong argument can be made ... that the government also has a compelling interest in protecting children from violent programming."*

The Government Has the Power to Regulate Violence on Television

Federal Communications Commission

The Federal Communications Commission (FCC) was established in 1934 as an independent government agency that answers to Congress. Its purpose is to regulate all broadcast media in the United States. In the following report issued at congressional request, the FCC argues that the national legislature probably has the power to regulate television violence by mandating that broadcasters restrict violent programming to specific times when children are less likely to be watching. The FCC bases its conclusion on judicial precedents and on the assumption that violent programming is of "slight social value" and therefore may

Federal Communications Commission, "Law and Policy Addressing the Distribution of Violent Television Programming," *In the Matter of Violent Television Programming and Its Impact on Children*, April 6, 2007.

not deserve full First Amendment protections. Although the FCC recommends strengthening other regulatory aids—such as V-chip controls and television content ratings—the commission contends that, so far, these protections have been ineffective in keeping children from violent programming.

As you read, consider the following questions:

1. According to the FCC, what was the ruling of the U.S. Court of Appeals for the District of Columbia in *Action for Children's Television v. FCC*?

2. In the FCC's view, why has the implementation of the V-chip proven to he an ineffective method of keeping children from violent or offensive programming?

3. According to the 2004 Kaiser survey quoted in the FCC viewpoint, what percentage of parents asserted that television programs are not rated accurately by the industry-devised ratings system?

Members of Congress asked the Commission to address the government's authority, consistent with the First Amendment, to restrict the broadcast or other distribution of excessively violent programming and what measures to constrain or regulate such programming are most likely to be sustained in court. Accordingly, we discuss below regulatory alternatives for protecting children from violent television content. We begin, however, with a brief overview of the relevant constitutional framework.

Violent speech and depictions of violence have been found by the courts to be protected by the First Amendment. However, [as the Supreme Court noted in the 1978 case *FCC v. Pacifica Foundation*] "each medium of expression presents special First Amendment problems," with broadcasting historically receiving "the most limited First Amendment protection." Thus, [as the Supreme Court concluded in the 1984 case *FCC v. League of Women Voters*] even when broadcast speech "lies at the heart of First Amendment protection," the government may regulate it so long as its interest in doing so is "substantial" and the restriction is "narrowly tailored" to further that interest. While a restriction on the content of protected speech will generally be upheld only if it satisfies strict scrutiny, meaning that the restriction must further a compelling government interest and be the least restrictive means to further that interest, this exacting standard does not apply to the regulation of broadcast speech.

In the realm of indecency, the U.S. Supreme Court has identified two principal reasons for the reduced First Amendment protection afforded to broadcasting: first, [quoting *Pacifica*] its "uniquely pervasive presence in the lives of all Americans;" and second, its accessibility to children, coupled with the government's interests in the well-being of children and in supporting parental supervision of children. In light of these characteristics, the Court, in *Pacifica*, upheld the Commission's authority to regulate the broadcast of indecent material. Relying on *Pacifica*, the U.S. Court of Appeals for the District of Columbia Circuit later concluded in [the 1995 case *Action for Children's Television v. FCC* (*ACT III*)] that the "channeling" of indecent content to the hours between 10:00 P.M. and 6:00 A.M. would not unduly burden First Amendment rights. It held that such regulation would promote the government's "compelling interest in supporting parental supervision of what children see and hear on the public airwaves." It also noted that it is "evident beyond the need for elaboration" that the government's "interest in safeguarding the physical and psychological well-being of a minor is compelling." In addition, in light of relevant U.S. Supreme Court precedent, the D.C. Circuit refused in *ACT III* to insist on scientific evidence that indecent content harms children, concluding that the government's interest in the well-being of minors is not "limited to protecting them from clinically measurable injury."

Restricting Violent Programming to Specific Times

Time Channeling. As stated above, members of Congress asked the Commission to address possible measures to protect children from excessively violent television content. We begin by discussing time channeling restrictions that would restrict such programming to hours when children are less likely to be in the viewing audience. We note that commenters disagreed about the constitutionality of such requirements. Pappas [Telecasting Companies] argued that they would be likely to pass constitutional muster because the government interests are substantially the same as those at stake in regulating broadcast indecency. Other commenters maintain that such requirements would be unconstitutional and unworkable.

After carefully evaluating these comments and relevant precedent, we find that Congress could impose time channeling restrictions on excessively violent television programming in a constitutional manner. Just as the government has a compelling interest in protecting children from sexually explicit programming, a strong argument can be made ... that the government also has a compelling interest in protecting children from violent programming and supporting parental supervision of minors' viewing of violent programming. We also believe that, if properly defined, excessively violent programming, like indecent programming, occupies a relatively low position in the hierarchy of First Amendment values because it is of "'slight social value as a step to truth'" [*Pacifica*]. Such programming is entitled to reduced First Amendment protection because of its pervasiveness and accessibility to children pursuant to the U.S. Supreme Court's reasoning in *Pacifica*.

Proving the Need for Time Channeling

To be sure, the government, when imposing time channeling, would have to show that such regulation is a narrowly tailored means of vindicating its interests in promoting parental supervision and protecting children. In this regard, however, we note that while the alternative measures discussed below—viewer-initiated blocking and mandatory ratings—would impose lesser burdens on protected speech, we are skeptical that they will fully serve the government's interests in promoting parental supervision and protecting the well-being of minors. In addition to these measures, as discussed below, another way of providing consumers greater control—and therefore greater ability to avoid violent programming—could be to require video channels to be offered on an "à la carte" basis [instead of in package deals that may contain unwanted channels with offensive programming]. As the D.C. Circuit has noted in the context of indecency: "It is fanciful to believe that the vast majority of parents who wish to shield their children from indecent material can effectively do so without meaningful restrictions on the airing of broadcast indecency [ACT III]." To cite just some of the relevant data, 81 percent of children ages two through seven sometimes watch television without adult supervision, and 91 percent of children ages four through six have turned on the television by themselves. In addition, as discussed below, the studies and surveys conducted to date tend to show that blocking technologies and the associated TV ratings system are of limited effectiveness in supporting parental supervision of minors' viewing habits.

Generally, however, the sustainability of time channeling restrictions would depend on a number of specific evidentiary considerations. Therefore, should Congress wish to adopt time channeling restrictions, lawmakers should make specific findings to support such restrictions. Significant issues that Congress may wish to address include the nature of the harm to children inflicted by violent television content, how to define such content, and the ages of the children that the government is seeking to protect. For example, indecent material is channeled to the hours between 10:00 P.M. and 6:00 A.M. This "safe harbor" is based on evidence that children 17 years of age and under are less likely to be in the audience during these hours. With respect to violent program content, the research suggests that younger children are most at risk, possibly requiring a different conclusion as to the ages of children to be protected and the appropriate "safe harbor" hours.

Weaknesses of Existing Regulatory Aids

Viewer-Initiated Blocking and Mandatory Ratings. Besides time channeling, another possible means of protecting children from violent television content is to strengthen mechanisms that enable viewer-initiated blocking of such content. In 1996, Congress amended Title III of the Communications Act to require the incorporation of blocking technology into television sets. As of January 1, 2000, all television sets manufactured in the United States or shipped in interstate commerce with a picture screen of thirteen inches or larger must be equipped with a "V-chip" system that can be programmed to block violent, sexual, or other programming that parents do not wish their children to view. However, out of a total universe of 280 million sets in U.S. households, only about 119 million sets in use today, or less than half, are equipped with V-chips.

Based on the studies and surveys conducted to date, we believe that the evidence clearly points to one conclusion: the V-chip is of limited effectiveness in protecting children from violent television content. In order for V-chip technology to block a specific category of television programming, such as violent content, it must be activated. However, many parents do not even know if the television sets in their households incorporate this technology and, of those who do, many do not use it. In 2004, the Kaiser Family Foundation conducted a telephone survey of 1,001 parents of children ages 2–17. The results showed: (1) only 15 percent of all parents have used the V-chip; (2) 26 percent of all parents have not bought a new television set since January 2000 (when the V-chip was first required in *all* sets); (3) 39 percent of parents have bought a new television set since January 2000, but do not think it includes a V-chip; and (4) 20 percent of parents know they have a V-chip, but have not used it. According to a 2003 study, parents' low level of V-chip use is explained in part by parents' unawareness of the device and the "multi-step and often confusing process" necessary to use it. Only 27 percent of parents in the study group could figure out how to program the V-chip, and many parents "who might otherwise have used the V-chip were frustrated by an inability to get it to work properly." A March 2007 Zogby poll indicates, among other things, that 88 percent of respondents did not use a V-chip or cable box parental controls in the previous week, leading the Parents Television Council to call the television industry's V-chip education campaign "a failure."

In addition to mandating inclusion of V-chip technology in television sets, the Act provides cable subscribers with some ways to block unwanted programming. These provisions of the Act, however, do not benefit households receiving their television programming via over-the-air broadcasting or satellite. Further, similar to the V-chip, to take advantage of these measures a cable subscriber first must be aware of and then affirmatively request that such measures be employed. Finally, to receive these protections, a cable subscriber must take several steps and incur some costs.

Specifically, while cable operators provide their digital subscribers with advanced parental control technology, those parental controls only are available to digital cable subscribers using digital cable set-top boxes. Of the cable industry's 65,600,000 subscriber households, only 32,602,000—less than half of all subscribers—subscribe to digital service. Furthermore, while those digital cable households likely have at least one cable operator-provided digital set-top box, many, if not most, of those homes do not have digital set-top boxes connected to every television used to view cable programming. Accordingly, the percentage of cable-connected television sets on which those advanced parental controls are available likely is even lower than the percentage of cable households that subscribe to digital cable services. Therefore, it does not appear that cable operator-provided advanced parental controls are available on a sufficient number of cable-connected television sets to be considered an effective solution at this time.

We believe that further action to enable viewer-initiated blocking of violent television content would serve the government's interests in protecting the well-being of children and facilitating parental supervision and would be reasonably likely to be upheld as constitutional. As indicated above, however, reliance on blocking technology alone would probably not fulfill the government's interest in protecting the well-being of children. Blocking technology does not ensure that children are prevented from viewing violent programming unless it is activated, and courts have recognized the practical limits of parental supervision.

Flaws in the Rating System

In addition, any successful viewer-initiated blocking regime with respect to violent programming would depend upon the adoption and successful implementation of an effective ratings system. Currently, to facilitate operation of the V-chip and other blocking mechanisms, broadcast, cable, and satellite television providers, on a voluntary basis, rate programming using the industry-devised TV ratings system guidelines and encode programs accordingly. Most television programming, except for news and sports programming, carries an age-based TV rating set by program networks and producers, and most include content-based ratings as well.

Studies and surveys demonstrate, however, that the voluntary TV ratings system is of limited effectiveness in protecting children from violent television content. In the 2004 Kaiser survey discussed above, 50 percent of all parents surveyed stated that they have used the TV ratings. But about 4 in 10

Parents Show Concern over Television Violence

Percent of parents who say they are most concerned about inappropriate content in:

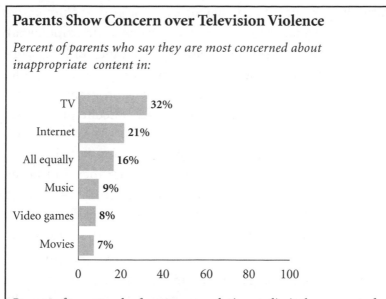

Percent of parents who favor new regulations to limit the amount of sex and violence in TV shows during the early evening hours:

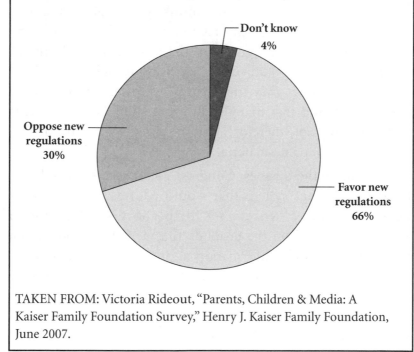

TAKEN FROM: Victoria Rideout, "Parents, Children & Media: A Kaiser Family Foundation Survey," Henry J. Kaiser Family Foundation, June 2007.

parents (39 percent) stated that most programs are not rated accurately, and many parents did not fully understand what the various ratings categories mean. For example, only 24 percent of parents of young children (two–six years old) could name any of the ratings that would apply to programming appropriate for children that age. Only 12 percent of parents knew that the rating FV ("fantasy violence") is related to violent content, while 8 percent thought it meant "family viewing." One in five (20 percent) parents said that they had never heard of the TV ratings system, an increase from 14 percent in 2000 and 2001. A more recent survey indicates that only 8 percent of respondents could correctly identify the categories.

And, of course, ratings can only be effective in protecting children from inappropriate content if the parent understands the ratings information, and such information is accurate. In a study published in the journal *Pediatrics*, parents concluded that half of television shows the industry had rated as appropriate for teenagers were in fact inappropriate, a finding the study authors called "a signal that the ratings are misleading." Academics who have studied the television rating system share parents' assessment that the ratings are often inaccurate. A 2002 study found that many shows that should carry content descriptors do not, therefore leaving parents unaware of potentially objectionable material. . . .

To address these issues, Congress could seek to establish a mandatory ratings system that would address the shortcomings of the current system set forth above. Such a system could be defended on the grounds that it merely requires the disclosure of truthful information about a potentially harmful product (violent television programming), thereby advancing the compelling government interests without significantly burdening First Amendment rights. It could also be defended as a necessary predicate for the operation of a successful system of viewer-initiated blocking. As stated above, however, although mandatory television ratings would impose lesser burdens on protected speech, we believe the evidence demonstrates that they would not fully serve the government's interest in the well-being of minors given the limits of parental supervision recognized by the D.C. Circuit in *ACT III*. Experience also leads us to question whether such a ratings system would ever be sufficiently accurate given the myriad of practical difficulties that would accompany any comprehensive effort to ensure the accuracy of ratings. Moreover, such a requirement may have an unintended practical consequence. There is some evidence that TV ratings may actually serve to attract certain underage viewers to programming that is violent or is otherwise labeled as not intended for a child audience.

> "Even assuming that the proponents of
> government control are right about how
> television violence affects young chil-
> dren, regulations addressing those ef-
> fects would be too ineffectual to pass
> constitutional muster."

The Government Should Not Regulate Violence on Television

Laurence H. Tribe

In the following viewpoint, Laurence H. Tribe, a professor of constitutional law at Harvard and the author of the seminal textbooks on the subject, insists that any attempt by the government to restrict or regulate television violence would violate the constitutional protection of free speech. Tribe asserts that given the variety of violence on television, the government could not hope to establish criteria to determine what would and would not be permissible for broadcast. In addition, Tribe contends that while these regulations may aim to protect young children, limiting violent programming would impinge on the right of adults and older children to have "unhindered access to uncensored

speech." Tribe concludes that ultimately such regulation is un-
necessary because parents already have options to restrict what
their children see and hear.

As you read, consider the following questions:

1. How does Tribe use the Old Testament and *Hamlet* to
   help further his argument against government censorship?
2. In Tribe's view, how would time channeling of television
   violence adversely affect households without children?
3. What does Tribe argue is the "right response" for government to pursue in helping to limit children's access
   to televised violence?

This week [in late June 2007], Congress turns once again to
the question of how to respond to the perceived threat of
television violence to the development and behavior of children. Under our Constitution, the proper response is plain,
even though it is not simple: give parents more power to control what their children see. But Congress's attention at this
time seems instead to signal an intent to involve the Federal
Government more deeply in what we are allowed to see on
our television sets. The FCC [Federal Communications Com-
mission], for instance, has suggested that Congress "time channel" certain shows to late night time slots or implement a
government-run ratings system. Such attempts to restrict free
speech would be grave mistakes—and ones that the courts are
unlikely to tolerate.

It's worth remembering that depictions of violence have
long played an important and respected role in all media of
expression. That a television program includes violent content
does not—and cannot—automatically trump its positive value
to society, or the inestimable value of resisting government
censorship. The Old Testament and the Koran are often violent; so are *Hamlet* and *The Call of the Wild;* and so are many

of our most beloved and acclaimed television shows, from "Mission Impossible" to "Law and Order" to broadcast and cable news networks' coverage of terrorist attacks and the Iraq war. Depictions of violence and its consequences can contribute powerfully to a show's portrayal of our often violent world and its equally violent history, and the use of violence—however disquieting—adds meaning that is nearly impossible to achieve otherwise.

How to Define What Is Excessive Violence

Even the staunchest critics of television violence must concede that only certain types of depicted violence cause real concern. But letting the government decide *which* depictions threaten children's welfare and should be so labeled or otherwise restricted is both unconstitutional and unwise. For one thing, any definition of "impermissibly" or "gratuitously" violent television programming will be "so vague that men of common intelligence must necessarily guess at its meaning and differ as to its application"—a violation of "the first essential of due process of law," as the Supreme Court held more than eighty years ago [in *Connally v. General Construction Co.* (1926)]. What possible criteria could determine whether the strenuous physical interrogation of a suspect on "24" is "patently offensive," or whether a gruesome depiction of the storming of Normandy [i.e., the D-Day invasion of World War II] is "excessive," to test just two proposed definitions?

Vague laws on any subject are unconstitutional, but such regulations are particularly troubling when directed at speech. The inevitable consequence of such vagueness is that valuable expression will be "chilled" as individuals and institutions try to avoid any speech that puts them at risk of being penalized for violating the law—even if that speech is not, in fact, illegal. And, on the other side of the enforcement coin, vague laws give regulators and prosecutors so much leeway that they can easily restrict speech "to pursue their own personal predilections" or to bow to political pressure rather than to implement faithfully the intent of Congress. [In early June 2007] the U.S. Court of Appeals for the Second Circuit ... raised just these concerns while striking down the FCC's attempts to fine broadcasters for "fleeting expletives" uttered on their shows.

Turning the First Amendment on Its Head

The dangers of boundless discretion are exacerbated by the fact that regulation of televised violence invariably responds less to the violent content itself than to what particular depictions *say* about the use of violence or what *attitudes toward violence* these depictions convey. But the First Amendment clearly prohibits government regulation based on the viewpoint expressed by speech. Congress cannot, for instance, restrict only speech that criticizes the government, while permitting pro-government speech. Similarly, Congress has no power to target speech that expresses a disapproved message about or attitude toward violence (such as a show that admiringly portrays a mobster's violent rise through the ranks) while leaving untouched "approved" speech on the same subject (such as a show condemning a drug dealer's violent retaliations).

Lawmakers may be tempted to relax these standards when the speech is restricted with the welfare of children in mind, but doing so would turn the First Amendment on its head. If anything, the degree to which children are especially impressionable cuts *against* letting the central government control what our children see or learn. Why else fight so hard over the teaching of evolution or the inclusion of "one Nation under God" in the pledge schoolchildren recite? And, even if the purpose of regulating television violence would be to protect young children, any such regulation would necessarily deprive adults and older children of unhindered access to uncensored speech. Time channeling, for instance, would prevent *everybody* from watching televised violence except during specified times—even in the large majority of television households without any young children. The First Amendment forbids limiting adults to speech that would be suitable for youngsters.

Finally, even assuming that the proponents of government control are right about how television violence affects young children, regulations addressing those effects would be too ineffectual to pass constitutional muster. The Supreme Court has held that a regulation of speech must "advance its asserted interests in [a] direct and material way" [*Edenfeld v. Fane* (1993)]. But the proponents' asserted interests are too at odds with one another to meet this requirement. The stated interest in protecting children from frightening material, for example, would suggest that any depiction of violence should be cartoonish and sanitized; but this would undercut the asserted interests in making children understand the consequences of violence and in avoiding material that the proponents of control fear children might imitate. And even the strongest of those proponents are likely to tolerate violence on such television programming as news and sports, even though these exceptions seem just as likely—or more likely, given their real-world nature—to cause the same effects as would the depictions of violence that some seek to prohibit.

Parents Have Options to Limit What Their Children Watch or Hear

In raising these First Amendment concerns, I do not mean to deny the legitimate concerns of parents about what their children see on television. As a father and a grandfather, I share those concerns. But it is also in my role as a parent and grandparent—even more than as a constitutional scholar—that I address them here. As parents, we should resist, not embrace, moves by government to control the upbringing of our chil-

The Right Role for Congress

Like most Americans—and most people in my industry—I'm concerned about what our kids see on television. I believe that Congress should take a leadership role in promoting technological innovation and informational initiatives to allow parents and the broadcasting industry to meet their responsibilities toward our children.

I would also support Congress funding research (research that adheres to strict scientific protocols) into the relationship between violent programming and aggressive behavior. I agree with you that dialogue and education are the key. But like most Americans, I don't want Congress censoring what I can or can't watch.

Parents presently have the most powerful screening tool in their hands—the "off" button on their remote. Networks are acutely sensitive to market pressures. Low ratings for an objectionable program will get it zapped quicker than any legislation.

Rene Balcer,
Wall Street Journal, *May 21, 2007.*

dren. We should insist on measures intended solely to facilitate *parental* control. The Supreme Court has repeatedly recognized that such measures are more narrowly tailored and less restrictive of speech, and case after case has obligated Congress to resort to such measures even when centralized government regulation would arguably have been more effective.

Fortunately, parents today have more options than ever before to control what their children see on television, from the V-chip to time-shifting technologies to voluntary ratings systems. To the extent that Congress worries about the effectiveness of these alternatives, the right response is to improve their distribution through publicity campaigns or government aid, not to bypass them on the easy path to censorship.

As with most policy questions that concern our children, the issue of whether and how to respond to television violence is difficult. It may seem easiest simply to delegate these decisions to the government. But the First Amendment demands that we as parents take responsibility for controlling what our children see or hear. Only by undertaking that duty can we protect our children—not just from inappropriate speech, but from a system of government that treads too readily on their constitutional rights.

> *"Public officials should not act in* loco parentis *when parents have the power to make media decisions on their own."*

Parents Should Regulate Their Children's Exposure to Violence on Television

Adam Thierer

Adam Thierer is a senior fellow and director of the Center for Digital Media Freedom at the Progress & Freedom Foundation, a think tank that studies digital age technology and its implications on public policy. In the following viewpoint, he argues that the government has no business regulating children's access to violence on television. That job, he claims, is best left to parents. Thierer explains that many new technologies are available to help parents limit their children's exposure to television violence. Signal blockers can keep children from accessing unapproved channels, and other devices can restrict available viewing times to certain hours of the day. Above all, however, Thierer maintains that the establishment of specific media rules in each household gives parents the greatest power over what their children watch.

As you read, consider the following questions:

1. According to Thierer, what kind of logic drove the U.S. Supreme Court's 1978 *FCC v. Pacifica* decision?
2. According to Thierer's quotation of Census Bureau statistics, what fraction of U.S. households include children under 18?
3. As Thierer describes it, what is the Parents Television Council and what does it do?

On April 25th [2007], the Federal Communications Commission (FCC) released its long-awaited report on "Violent Television Programming and Its Impact on Children." The report recommends that "action should be taken to address violent programming" on both broadcast, over-the-air television as well as subscription-based cable and satellite systems. The FCC report suggests that Congress could apply traditional indecency restrictions to violent programming on broadcast TV and that cable and satellite operators should be forced to sell their programming on an "à la carte" (channel-by-channel) basis in an attempt to eradicate violent programming from pay TV.

There is a better way to regulate media violence than through government mandates. Parents have the power to regulate the media in their lives and the lives of their children. And technical controls like the V-chip and set-top box controls are only one part of that process. Informal household media rules and third-party-provided content ratings and program information are equally as important.

Public officials should not act *in loco parentis* [in place of a parent] when parents have the power to make media decisions on their own. Raising children, and determining what type of media they consume, is a quintessential parental responsibility. This [viewpoint] will outline the many tools and methods—both technical and non-technical—that parents have at their disposal to carry out this task.

Why Not Regulate?

This [viewpoint] will not dwell on the many thorny constitutional issues raised by proposals to regulate "violent" fare on television. It is important for lawmakers to realize, however, that the courts will likely take a very skeptical look at any proposal to regulate something as nebulous as "excessive violence" on television. In fact, in recent years, the thrust of First Amendment-related jurisprudence has all been strongly tending toward greater freedom of speech and away from government intervention. This makes parental control tools and methods more important than ever before.

In the past, the "off" button on television sets or remote controls was the only technical control at a parent's disposal. In that environment, many believed that government needed to act as surrogate for parents because of the lack of control families had over their media decisions/encounters. In other words, because it was difficult for families to enforce their own "household standard," the government would step in and create a baseline—but quite amorphous and sometimes completely arbitrary—"community standard" for the entire nation. And that community standard would be enforced by law and treat all households as if they had the same tastes or values.

This was the logic that drove the famous 1978 [*FCC v.*] *Pacifica* decision in which the Supreme Court held that FCC oversight and regulatory penalties (i.e., fines or license revocation) would help prevent "uninvited" programming from acting as an "intruder" into the home. By a slim 5–4 margin, that logic became the law of the land for broadcast "indecency" and remains so today.

But when similar arguments were put forward by policymakers in the mid-1990s in defense of restrictions on Internet and video game content, courts rejected those efforts. In striking down the Communications Decency Act of 1996, which sought to apply indecency regulation to Internet websites, the

Supreme Court declared in *Reno v. ACLU* (1996) that a law that places a "burden on adult speech is unacceptable if less restrictive alternatives would be at least as effective in achieving" the same goal. Several lower courts (including two federal appellate courts) have rejected regulation of video game content on similar grounds.

What is most interesting about these recent Internet and video game decisions is that the same logic could be applied to many other types of media outlets and content—including broadcast and cable TV. Indeed, there are many "less restrictive alternatives" available to parents today to help them shield their children's eyes and ears from content they might find objectionable, including violently themed content.

If it is the case that families now have the ability to effectively tailor media consumption to their own preferences—that is, to craft their own "household standard"—the regulatory equation for television will likely also change eventually. In essence, the courts are saying that regulation can no longer be premised upon the supposed helplessness of households to deal with content flows if families have been empowered to make content determinations for themselves. . . .

This is why parental control tools and methods are more important than ever before. The courts have largely foreclosed government censorship and placed responsibility over what enters the home squarely in the hands of parents.

And that is how it should be. Decisions about acceptable media content are extraordinarily personal; no two people or families will have the same set of values, especially in a nation as diverse as ours. Consequently, it would be optimal if public policy decisions in this field took into account the extraordinary diversity of citizen/household tastes and left the ultimate decision about acceptable content to them. That's especially the case in light of the fact that most U.S. households are made up entirely of adults. According to the Census Bureau, only one-third of U.S. households include children under the age of 18.

Importantly, household-based controls need not be perfect to be preferable to government controls. That is particularly true because of the First Amendment values at stake in this debate. Absent removing all media devices from a home, it would be impossible to eliminate all unwanted or unexpected encounters from life. Parental control tools and methods will not always provide perfect protection, but they can act as training wheels or speed bumps along the media paths that children seek to go down *without destroying those paths altogether as government censorship would do.*

What follows is a description of the many tools and methods that parents have at their disposal today to deal with potentially objectionable media content, including televised programming that includes violent themes or images. These tools and methods will be divided into two categories—(1) technical tools and methods, and (2) non-technical tools and methods—and described in detail. . . .

These age-based ratings and content descriptors appear in the upper left hand corner of the screen at the start of each television program. If the program is more than one hour, the icon will reappear at the beginning of the second hour. The ratings and descriptors also appear on the TV's on-screen menus and interactive guides, on the TV networks' Web sites, and in local newspaper or *TV Guide* listings. This information is also encoded and embedded into each TV program so that the V-chip or other devices can screen and filter by ratings.

The FCC also hosts a Web site that provides detailed instruction regarding how to use the V-chip. "TV Watch," a coalition of media experts and media organizations, provides a Web site with tutorials and tool kits to help parents program the V-chip and find other tools to control television in the home. And a new industry sponsored campaign entitled "The

The V-chip & TV Ratings

As a standard feature in all televisions 13″ and larger built after January 2000, the V-chip gives households the ability to screen televised content by ratings that are affixed to almost all programs. The V-chip can be accessed through the setup menus on televisions, or often is just one click away using a designated button on the TV's remote. Households can then use password-protected blocking to filter programs by rating. The ratings system, available online at www.tvguidelines.org/ratings.asp, offers the following age-based designations (Table 1):

Table 1: TV Ratings

TV-Y	All Children
TV-Y7	Directed to Children Age 7 and Older
TV-Y7 (FV)	Directed to Older Children Due to Fantasy Violence
TV-G	General Audience
TV-PG	Parental Guidance Suggested
TV-14	Parents Strongly Cautioned
TV-MA	Mature Audience Only

The TV ratings system also uses several content descriptors to better inform parents and all viewers about the nature of the content they will be experiencing. These content descriptors include (Table 2):

Table 2: TV Content Descriptors

D	Suggestive Dialogue
L	Coarse Language
S	Sexual Situations
V	Violence
FV	Fantasy Violence

TV Boss" offers easy-to-understand tutorials explaining how to program the V-chip or cable and satellite set-top box controls. As part of the effort, several PSAs and other advertisements have aired or been published reminding parents that these capabilities are at their disposal. . . .

Cable & Satellite TV Controls

With roughly 86 percent of U.S. households subscribing to cable or satellite television systems today, the tools that these multichannel video programming providers offer to subscribers are a vital part of the parental controls mix today. Parental controls are usually just one button-click away on most cable and satellite remote controls and boxes.

Both analog and digital boxes allow parents to block individual channels and lock them using passwords so that children can't access them. Newer, digital boxes offer more extensive filtering capabilities that allow programs to be blocked by rating, channel, or title. Some systems even allow users to block the program descriptions on the interactive guide (for adult pay-per-view programming, for example) if families don't want them to be visible.

For cable subscribers that do not have set-top boxes, they can request that cable companies take steps to block specific channels for them. A comprehensive survey of the content controls that cable television providers make available to their subscribers can be found on the National Cable and Telecommunications Association's (NCTA) "Control Your TV" Web site. Aftermarket solutions are also available that allow parents to block channels. The "TV Channel Blocker" gives households the ability to block any analog cable channel between channels 2–86, including broadcast stations carried by the cable operator. The unit can be self-installed by homeowners on the wall where the cable line enters the home. It can then block specific channels on any television in the home. . . .

Satellite providers DirecTV and EchoStar's Dish Network also offer extensive parental control tools via their set-top boxes. And telephone companies, such as AT&T and Verizon are also getting into the video distribution business and offering similar tools. Many of the same set-top boxes deployed by the cable industry are used by these telco providers. Therefore, the parental control capabilities are quite similar.

Some multichannel operators also offer subscribers the option of buying a bundle of "family-friendly" channels. For example, Dish Network offers a "Family Pak" and DirecTV offers a "Family Choice" bundle of channels. Many cable operators offer similar bundles, but parents must consult their local provider to get details since packages vary by zip code or county. Major cable operators such as Comcast, Time Warner, Cox, Insight Communications, Mid-Continent, and Bright House all offer family packages. Also, a unique satellite service called Sky Angel offers 33 channels of what it describes as "Christ-centered & family-friendly choice(s)" that households can subscribe to if they only want religious programming available in their homes.

Other Hardware Controls

One of the most important developments on the parental controls front in recent years has been the rapid rise and diffusion of VCRs, DVD players, personal video recorders (PVRs), and home computers. These technologies give parents the ability to accumulate libraries of preferred programming for their children and determine exactly when it will be viewed. This can help parents tailor programming to their specific needs and values. If certain parents believed that their children should only be raised solely on reruns of "The Lone Ranger" and "Leave it to Beaver," then these new media technologies can make it happen! . . .

But for those families that want to block out televised programming aired during certain hours of the day or limit how much TV can be viewed at all, technological tools exist that can make that possible. The Family Safe Media.com Web site sells a half dozen "TV time management" tools that allow parents to restrict the time of day or aggregate number of hours that children watch programming. Most of these devices, such as the "Bob TV Timer" by Hopscotch Technology and the "TV Allowance" television time manager, feature PIN-activated security methods and tamper-proof lock boxes that make it impossible for children to unplug or reset the device. Parents can use these devices to establish a daily or weekly "allowance" of TV or game screen time and then let children determine how to allocate it. . . . Similarly, "credit-based" devices such as the "Play Limit" box require that children place time tokens in a metallic lock box to determine how much TV time is allowed. Parents can provide a certain allowance of tokens to restrict the overall amount of screen time.

Non-Technical Tools & Methods

The technological tools and controls discussed above allow parents to automate the filtering/blocking process in their homes. While not perfect, they allow households to effectively tailor family viewing to their own unique preferences. Equally as important, however—and quite often overlooked—are the formal and informal household "media rules" and informal parental control methods that almost all families utilize.

In fact, in many ways, these non-technical household efforts represent the most important steps that parents can take to deal with potentially objectionable content or teach their children or how to be sensible, savvy media consumers. Indeed, to the extent that many households never take advantage of the many technical controls discussed above, it is likely because they instead rely on the many informal rules and methods discussed below.

Household Media Consumption Rules

To begin, there are formal and informal household "media consumption rules." A 2003 Kaiser Family Foundation survey found that "Almost all parents say they have some type of rules about their children's use of media." And a 2006 Kaiser survey of families with infants and preschoolers revealed that 85 percent of those parents who let their children watch TV at that age have rules about what their child can and cannot watch. 63 percent of those parents say they enforce those rules all of the time. About the same percentage of parents said they had similar rules for video game and computer usage. . . .

Pressure Media Providers to Make Changes

Parents can also work with other others to influence media content before it comes into the home, or rely on other groups they trust to help them better understand what is in the media they are considering bringing into the home.

Parents can pressure media providers and programmers directly through public campaigns, or indirectly through advertisers. Groups like the Parents Television Council, Morality in Media, Common Sense Media, and the National Institute on Media and the Family can play a constructive role in influencing content decisions through the pressure they can collectively bring to bear on media providers in the marketplace.

For example, Morality in Media's Web site outlines several strategies parents can use to influence advertisers, programming executives, and cable operators before resorting to calls for censorship. To allow parents to pressure advertisers, the group publishes a book listing the top 100 national advertisers, with addresses, phone and fax numbers, names of key executives, and their products, along with a products list cross-referenced to the manufacturer. The group produces a similar book that lists the names and addresses of the CEOs of the leading broadcast and cable companies in America so that viewers or listeners can complain directly to them. Similarly, the Parents Television Council (PTC) awards its "parent's seal of approval" to advertisers who only support programs that the PTC classifies as family-friendly. PTC also encourages parents to write letters and send e-mails to advertisers who support programming they find objectionable and encourage those advertisers to end their support of those shows. . . .

Inaction Should Not Justify Government Regulation

The combination of the V-chip, set-top box parental controls, various ratings systems, and other screening tools (personal video recorders in particular) mean that parents now have multiple layers of technological protection at their disposal. . . .

More importantly, almost all parents enforce a variety of household media rules and have guidelines for acceptable media consumption. These informal rules and strategies are an essential part of the parental controls story, but they are almost completely overlooked in public policy debates about these issues.

Of course, whether or not parents are taking advantage of any of these tools or options is another matter entirely. But if, for whatever reason, some parents are not taking advantage of these tools and options, their inaction should not be used to justify government regulation of programming as a surrogate for household/parental choice. Parents have been empowered. It is now their responsibility to take advantage of the parental control tools and methods at their disposal to determine what is acceptable for their families.

> "We should trust parents to prioritize
> the risks to their otherwise well-padded
> offspring."

Parents Recognize That Regulating Violence on Television Is Unnecessary

Kerry Howley

In the following viewpoint, Kerry Howley, a senior editor at Reason *magazine, takes issue with the Federal Communications Commission's 2007 report that advocates imposing regulations on television violence. According to Howley, the government assumes that because parents are not widely using blocking devices and rating systems to limit the amount of violence their children see on television, parents simply do not understand these aids, and therefore congressionally imposed regulation is necessary. Howley counters that most parents do not use these devices because they do not agree with the assumption that television violence will corrupt their children. Howley states that though politicians warn of the supposed inundation of televised violence, violent crime has steadily decreased in America to a level equiva-*

lent to what the nation experienced before the invention of television. Concurring with parents who also recognize this fact, she insists that government attempts at regulation are wrongheaded.

As you read, consider the following questions:

1. According to the Zogby poll quoted in the viewpoint, what percentage of parents did not use the V-chip or other blocking device on their televisions?
2. Why does Howley say that television ratings systems and the V-chip are held to a higher standard than other marketed goods?
3. Why does Howley contend that television is not as powerful a force in children's lives as it once was?

"Violent Television Programming and Its Impact on Children," the Federal Communications Commission's [April 2007] report (pdf) on the need to regulate violence in television, fails to define *violence*, delineate the scope of what needs regulating, or explain how exactly dangerously-placed pixels will destroy the nation's children. The 39-page report, two years in the making, is clear on only one point: Parents are the "first and last line of defense" against violence in television, and that, in itself, is the problem.

Consider the V-chip, the blocking device that Congress demanded be installed in every new TV larger than 13 inches. Even more beguiling than the little-known on/off switch, this control module appears well beyond the understanding of most child-owning Americans. The report warns us that activating a V-chip is a "multi-step" process. Even worse, parents don't even seem to know that their televisions contain these devices. Thirty-nine percent of parents who own V-chips apparently think they don't. And blocking technology, the report helpfully explains, "does not ensure that children are prevented from viewing violent programming unless it is activated."

Youth Violence Continues to Decline

Exaggerated claims about the link between violent media content and real-world aggression are ... refuted by an examination of recent crime rate statistics. According to the federal government, violent crime rates have plummeted since the mid-1990s and have now reached 30-year lows. Youth violence and violence in school have also declined. But if the media critics who continually complain about purported increases in the amounts and intensity of violence depicted in the media were right, then violent crimes should have increased, rather than significantly decreased, in recent years. In sum, the available evidence simply does not support claims that exposure to television violence causes children or adults to be aggressive.

National Association of Broadcasters, comments before the Federal Communications Commission, October 15, 2004.

When it comes to the TV ratings system, parents don't fare much better. "Only 24 percent of parents of young children," explains the report, "could name any of the ratings that would apply to programming appropriate for children that age." In 2001, 14 percent of parents said they'd never heard of the TV ratings system; today, 20 percent say they've never heard of it. Twelve percent of parents knew that the rating FV stands for "fantasy violence"; 8 percent told researchers that it meant "family viewing."

The FCC Assumes Parents Just Do Not Understand Blocking Devices and Ratings

At this point in our story, you might expect the FCC to recommend that the act of childbearing require its imprimatur. But the FCC just thinks parents need ... help. Parents, writes

Commissioner Jonathan Adelstein in a most poetic report addendum, "are like 17th century sailors subject to the whims of an angry sea." FCC head Kevin Martin piles on, explaining that lost parent/sailors are legion. "Even parents who have TVs equipped with a V-chip need more help," he writes. "According to a recent Zogby poll, 88% of parents did not use a V-chip or a cable blocking device."

This is a curious leap of reasoning. When the public chooses not to use or consume some widely available good—the ill-fated Zune [MP3 player], for instance—we typically assume that consumer taste has been misjudged, the size of a potential market miscalculated. The V-chip and TV ratings system are held to a higher standard. Unlike the Zune, you're required to own the V-chip with the purchase of a new TV. And if you choose not to use the chip you had no choice but to buy, we're to assume you don't *understand* it.

There is another, more Occam-friendly explanation for parents' ignorance of ratings and chips, but it is in no one's interest to suggest that parents aren't particularly concerned about the effects of *Extreme Makeover* or *CSI*. Free speech groups who promote education and voluntary parental controls are invested in parental competence. Government officials who want to "help" parents by obviating the need for parental discretion must argue that their help is wanted. Both sides of the debate have adopted the rhetoric of parental empowerment, and they're both faced with a majority of parents who choose not to use the tools they're forced to buy. And so censorship advocates argue that parents are the true children, in want of the protection they're simply unable to provide.

Many Parents Do Not Agree with Assumptions About Media Violence

It's not that parents don't think media violence is benign in the abstract; when polled, they tend to express concern about its effects. It just doesn't seem to be *their* kids at issue. A similar dynamic seems to be at work in video game purchases. According to a [April 2007] Federal Trade Commission report, 90 percent of parents are aware of the game ratings system, and two thirds of parents always or usually agree with its determinations. Yet 40 percent of parents who know system report that they let their kids play games deemed Mature; nearly a quarter of kids named an M-rated game as a favorite.

Parents, adrift illiterates that they are, probably haven't perused many studies on media violence and child aggression, nor many meta-analyses assessing the state of that research. But perhaps they've already concluded, through the field experiment that is parenting, what skeptical researchers have long held: The link between televised violence and a violent society is extremely tenuous. It's a fact even the report's authors seem to have gathered, given their tepid description of the link. "We agree with the views of the Surgeon General and find that, on balance, research provides strong evidence that exposure to violence in the media can increase aggressive behavior in children, at least in the short term."

As University of Toronto psychologist Jonathan Freedman has argued, laboratory experiments that show such a link are highly problematic: The measures of aggression are analogues of questionable value, it is difficult to equate violent films with nonviolent films and tease out the effects of violence, and experiment subjects may simply exhibit the behaviors they think researchers want to see. And outside the lab? "Field experiments almost all fail to find any increase in aggression due to exposure to violent media," says Freedman. "There is nothing there."

Television Is Only a Part of Children's Experience

The report as a whole is oddly anachronistic, a throwback to an age when a box in the family room went unrivaled for a kid's attention. "Television is perhaps the most powerful force at work in the world today," writes commissioner Michael J. Copps, a statement at best meaningless and at worst misleading. How powerful a force is television in an *American child's* life? The report claims children spend between 2 and 4 hours in front of the television a day, but cites a study that puts the number at 1 for children up to age 6 and 13.6 hours per week for ages 13–24.

Such numbers mean very little on their own. Children experience television among a cacophony of other messages and mediums, from the Internet to radio to magazines to music to video games. Broadcast television doesn't even rule the small screen; cable, satellite, and DVDs compete for attention. Given the shrinking space broadcast occupies in a child's life, and the lack of any obvious connection between violent TV and violent kids, it should come as no surprise that parents have left their V-chips unactivated and the ratings system unstudied.

Perhaps we should trust parents to prioritize the risks to their otherwise well-padded offspring. Supposedly awash in media violence, kids are growing up in an America less violent than the one their parents knew. "Since 1990 there has been a tremendous drop in the rate of violent crime," says Freedman. "If the effects of violence are so great, you'd think the violent crime rate would go up. You'd think there would be an epidemic of crime, but it's dropped like a stone—and it's now down to where it was before television was invented."

> "Millions of parents rely on ESRB ratings to choose games they deem appropriate for their children and families, and we value greatly the trust they have placed in our ratings."

The Video Game Ratings System Is an Effective Regulation

Patricia E. Vance

Patricia E. Vance is the president of the Entertainment Software Rating Board (ESRB), a self-regulatory body established in 1994 by the Entertainment Software Association. In the following viewpoint, excerpted from her written testimony before a congressional subcommittee investigating violence in video games, Vance explains the function of the ESRB ratings system and how it seeks to advise parents on the content and age-level appropriateness of all video games. Vance states that the ESRB uses independent reviewers who have no ties to the game industry and are culturally diverse so that they better represent the overall national population. The ratings these reviewers assign reflect

Patricia E. Vance, "Written testimony: Violent and Explicit Video Games: Informing Parents and Protecting Children," Hearing before the U.S. House of Representatives Subcommittee on Commerce, Trade and Consumer Protection, June 14, 2006. Reproduced by permission of the author.

mainstream opinions well, according to Vance, and have been praised by parents as well as organizations concerned with child welfare.

As you read, consider the following questions:

1. According to Vance, what percentage of parents use the ESRB ratings when purchasing appropriate video games for their children?
2. As Vance states, how many games received a M (Mature) rating in 2005?
3. What sanctions did the ESRB place upon Rockstar Games when it was disclosed that its *Grand Theft Auto: San Andreas* game had downloadable, sexually explicit content?

The ESRB was created in 1994 to provide consumers, particularly parents, with the information they need to make informed computer and video game purchase decisions. The ESRB rating system was developed after consulting a wide range of child development and academic experts, analyzing other rating systems, and conducting nationwide research among parents. Through these efforts, ESRB found that what parents really wanted from a video game rating system were both age-based categories and, equally if not more importantly, objective and detailed information about what is in the game. Those surveyed agreed that a rating system should inform and suggest, not prohibit, and that the rating system should not attempt to quantify objectionable incidents, but instead should reflect the overall content and objective of the game.

Since its inception, the rating system has been periodically enhanced, revised and updated to not only ensure that we continue providing the best possible service to those who rely on the ratings, but also to keep pace with what is a rapidly evolving medium and industry. Today, we remain extremely proud of the ESRB rating system and the information it provides. We have assigned over 12,000.[1] ratings in our history, and average over a thousand a year. Millions of parents rely on ESRB ratings to choose games they deem appropriate for their children and families, and we value greatly the trust they have placed in our ratings.

The ESRB Rating System

Although voluntary, the rating system has been universally adopted by the game industry, and virtually all computer and video games sold in the U.S. today carry an ESRB rating. Based on the aforementioned research conducted in 1994, the ESRB rating system was created with two equally important parts:

- **rating symbols**, easily identifiable on the front of game packaging that suggest the most appropriate age group for each game, and

- **content descriptors**, found on the back, clearly stating why a game received a particular rating or indicating content that may be of interest or concern.

Rating Categories and Definitions

- **EARLY CHILDHOOD**—Titles rated EC (Early Childhood) have content that may be suitable for ages 3 and older. Contains no material that parents would find inappropriate.

- **EVERYONE**—Titles rated E (Everyone) have content that may be suitable for ages 6 and older. Titles in this category may contain minimal cartoon, fantasy or mild violence and/or infrequent use of mild language.

- **EVERYONE** 10+—Titles rated E10+ (Everyone 10 and older) have content that may be suitable for ages 10

1. As of June 2008 the ESRB had assigned over 15,000 ratings.

and older. Titles in this category may contain more cartoon, fantasy or mild violence, mild language, and/or minimal suggestive themes.

- **TEEN**—Titles rated T (Teen) have content that may be suitable for ages 13 and older. Titles in this category may contain violence, suggestive themes, crude humor, minimal blood, simulated gambling and/or infrequent use of strong language.

- **MATURE**—Titles rated M (Mature) have content that may be suitable for persons ages 17 and older. Titles in this category may contain intense violence, blood and gore, sexual content, and/or strong language.

- **ADULTS ONLY**—Titles rated AO (Adults Only) have content that should only be played by persons 18 years and older. Titles in this category may include prolonged scenes of intense violence and/or graphic sexual content and nudity.

Rating Category Breakdown

Though violent games tend to receive a disproportionately high amount of attention, the reality is that the vast majority of games rated by ESRB are appropriate for younger players. As a point of reference, of the 1,133 ratings assigned by the ESRB in 2005[2], 50% were rated E (Everyone), 12% were rated E10+ (Everyone ages 10 and up)[3], and 24% were rated T (Teen). Games rated M (Mature) represented 12% of rating assignments, with the EC (Early Childhood) and AO (Adults Only) categories comprising the remainder.

2. Of the 1,563 ratings assigned by ESRB in 2007, 59% were E (Everyone), 15% were E10+ (Everyone 10 and up), 20% were T (Teen) and 6% were M (Mature), with the EC (Early Childhood) and AO (Adults Only) categories composing the statistically insignificant remainder.
3. The E10+ rating category was introduced in March 2005.

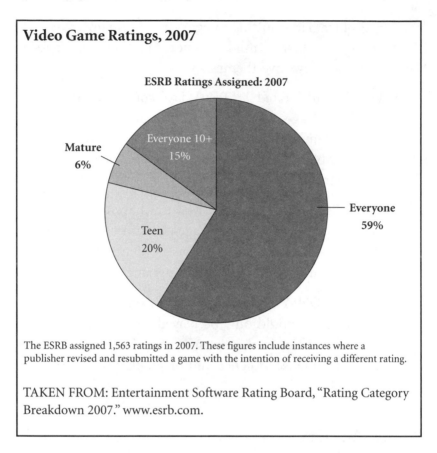

Video Game Ratings, 2007

ESRB Ratings Assigned: 2007

- Everyone 10+ 15%
- Mature 6%
- Everyone 59%
- Teen 20%

The ESRB assigned 1,563 ratings in 2007. These figures include instances where a publisher revised and resubmitted a game with the intention of receiving a different rating.

TAKEN FROM: Entertainment Software Rating Board, "Rating Category Breakdown 2007." www.esrb.com.

Pertinent Content

Pertinent content spans various categories including violence, profanity, sexual or suggestive content, depiction and/or use of controlled substances, gambling, etc. The following list explains what types of content are considered pertinent from a ratings standpoint:

- Destruction—Explosions and physical damage, including audio and visual elements of destruction

- Rewards/Penalties—Rewards, punishments, and penalties for certain player behavior, such as ending the game if the player attacks civilians

- Violence—All elements of damage design including blood effects, gore, death animations, post-mortem damage effects, and screams

- Failure—What happens when the player dies, crashes, or goes out-of-bounds

- Profanity—Any profanity and how often it occurs, whether it is spoken, gestured, or written in text

- Soundtrack/Lyrics—Soundtracks that contain profanity or adult themes, including edits or "bleeps," and lyric sheets

- Controlled Substances—Use, implied use, or reference to drugs, alcohol or tobacco, even in the background

- Gambling—Gambling, including instructional lessons or mere reference

- Sexuality—Sexually oriented and suggestive themes or dialogue, character models and dress, nudity, and explicit sexual activities/references

- Perspectives—Different game perspectives, such as first person, third person, top-down, etc.

- Sound Effects—Sound effects including those associated with pain, death, explosions, weapons, sexual activity, and bodily functions

- Weapons—Depictions of weapons and the different effects they produce

Rating Process[4]

Prior to a game being released to the public, game publishers submit a detailed written questionnaire to the ESRB, often with supplements (such as lyric sheets, scripts, etc.), specifying

4. The ESRB's transition to full-time raters in April 2007 also involved minor adjustments to the rating process. For a full description of the ESRB's current ratings process, please visit: www.esrb.org/ratings/ratings_process.jsp.

exactly what pertinent content will be in the final version of the game. Along with the written submission materials, publishers must provide a videotape capturing all pertinent content, incorporating the most extreme instances, across all relevant categories including but not limited to violence, language, sexual or suggestive, controlled substances and gambling. Pertinent content that is not programmed to be playable but will exist in the final game's code base must also be disclosed.

Once the submission is checked by ESRB for completeness, which may also involve ESRB staff members playing a beta version of the game, the video footage is reviewed by at least three or more raters. Upon independently reviewing the video, the raters recommend appropriate rating categories and content descriptors for the content in each scene reviewed and the game overall. Raters consider many elements in their assignments including context, realism, frequency, the reward system, the degree of player control and overall intensity, among others.

While some suggest that ESRB should play each video game as part of the rating process (play-testing does occur on a limited basis), there are several reasons why this would be impractical. First, since ESRB ratings must appear on game packaging and in all advertising when the product is released, we oftentimes receive games that are not yet fully playable from start to finish, or "buggy," at that point in the development process. Secondly, many games have upwards of 50 hours of gameplay, and so requiring raters to play each of the more than 1,000 games we rate each year would not only be inefficient and unnecessary considering the high degree of repetition in video games, but due to their length and complexity, would offer no greater assurance that ESRB raters would find and review all of the pertinent content.

Lastly, ESRB ratings are based on the consensus of independent raters whose values and judgment reflect those of the mainstream American public, especially parents (see Consumer Research below). Requiring all ESRB raters to be expert gamers (which they would need to be if the rating process depended on playing through every game submitted) may hinder the ESRB's ability to recruit a diverse rater pool that is reflective of mainstream public opinion.

For all of the above reasons, ESRB legally requires publishers to disclose all pertinent content in their game, including the most extreme, no matter how hidden and difficult to find, so that raters can and do assign an accurate rating.

ESRB Enforcement System

As the game industry's self-regulatory body, the ESRB is responsible for the enforcement of its rating system. The ESRB enforcement system has been praised by the U.S. Federal Trade Commission and several government leaders for its efficacy and comprehensiveness, setting it apart from other entertainment media rating systems in terms of its scope and severity. Companies who do not comply with ESRB guidelines are subject to a wide range of ESRB sanctions, including fines, corrective actions, and other penalties. In fact, a complete review of the ESRB enforcement system was recently completed with the expert counsel and support of prominent attorneys Eric Holder Jr., Partner with Covington & Burling and former U.S. Deputy Attorney General, and Joseph diGenova, Founding Partner with diGenova & Toensing, LLP, former U.S. Attorney for the District of Columbia and special counsel for some of the most highly visible governmental inquiries in recent history. Their review resulted in a new class of violations for an "egregious" failure to disclose pertinent content, carrying a fine up to $1,000,000, among other enhancements. A letter from both Mr. DiGenova and Mr. Holder, in which they state that the video game industry is "taking great care to protect consumers and to fulfill the responsibilities and obligations of its self-regulatory system," is attached for the consideration of this Subcommittee.

Ratings. Every publisher of a game rated by the ESRB is legally bound to disclose all pertinent content when submitting the game for an ESRB rating, including, as of July 2005, content that is programmed to be inaccessible and will remain "locked out" in the final code of the game. To ensure that all pertinent content was fully disclosed during the rating process, after a game is publicly released, ESRB testers review randomly and hand-selected final product. In the event that material that would have affected the assignment of a rating or content descriptor is found to have not been previously disclosed, the ESRB is empowered to impose corrective actions and a wide range of sanctions, including points, monetary fines up to $1 million for the most egregious offenses, and even suspension of rating services. Corrective actions can include pulling advertising until ratings information can be corrected, stickering packaging with correct ratings information, recalling the product, and other steps the publisher must take so the consumer has accurate information.

Last year, a widely publicized incident involving the game *Grand Theft Auto: San Andreas* showed how effective and forceful an enforcement system we have at our disposal. After ESRB confirmed that the game's publisher, Rockstar Games, had not disclosed sexually explicit content that was "locked out" in the code of the game[5] but which could be accessed if players downloaded from the Internet a modification (dubbed "Hot Coffee") created by a hacker, ESRB swiftly announced the revocation of the game's initial M (Mature) rating and re-rated it AO (Adults Only). Additionally, the publisher agreed to advise retailers to immediately cease sales of the game until all inventory in the retail channel could either be stickered with the AO rating, or existing copies could be exchanged for new versions without the locked-out content, maintaining the original M rating. Further, the publisher agreed to make avail-

---

5. At the time that *Grand Theft Auto: San Andreas* was submitted for rating, ESRB's published submission rules did not require the disclosure of "locked-out" content.

able on the Internet a patch for parents to download which would make the modification inoperable on the PC version of the game. I submit that there is no other industry self-regulatory system willing or capable of imposing such swift and sweeping sanctions on its own members, which in this particular case resulted in the removal of a top-selling product from the market and a major loss of sales.

Opportunistic activists with their own agendas capitalized on the issue by casting "Hot Coffee" as evidence of a broken rating system and turning it into a political football. However, the facts make it abundantly clear that the actions taken by ESRB are strong evidence of an extremely capable self-regulatory body. In 30 days, the ESRB had thoroughly investigated a complex and unprecedented situation affecting one of the most popular video games ever released, had assessed the implications and scope of the content and its availability, changed its policies regarding disclosure requirements for locked-out content, and imposed prudent corrective actions on the publisher that effectively removed a top-selling product from the marketplace. These actions were taken with the interest of consumers and their trust in the ratings as our highest priority.

Consumer Research

In order to ensure that the ratings assigned by ESRB reflect the standards and meet the expectations of average American consumers, we conduct consumer research on an annual basis in ten different markets across the U.S. This research has consistently shown that parents overwhelmingly agree with the ratings that we apply. Peter D. Hart Research Associates, a nationally renowned independent opinion research firm, tests randomly selected video games rated during the prior 12 months with parents of children between the ages of 6 and 17. Parents are shown clips of actual game footage and then asked what rating they would apply. They are then asked to compare their own rating to the one actually assigned by the ESRB and whether they agree with it. Last year, this research found that parents agreed, or even thought our ratings were too strict, 87% of the time. Parents described the actual ratings as "about right" in 82% of all instances and "too strict" 5% of the time.

That said, ratings are only effective if they are being used, and so ESRB also commissions annual research of ratings awareness and use. In our most recent study conducted in March 2006[6], 83% of parents surveyed were aware of the ESRB ratings (up from 78% in 2005) and 74% use them regularly when choosing games for their families (up from 70% in 2005). Awareness of content descriptors also continues to grow, and is now at 65% (up from 61% in 2005). Fifty-three percent (53%) of parents "never" allow their children to play M-rated games and 41% "sometimes" do. Parents of kids under the age of 13 are almost twice as likely to "never" allow their children to play an M-rated game. Fully 91% of respondents indicated that they trust the ESRB ratings, saying their trust has either stayed "about the same" (76%) or increased (15%) during the past year. Other opinion polls conducted by Hart Research show that parents not only agree with specific ESRB ratings, but that 90% of them say the ESRB rating system provides the kind of information they need.

Consumer Education & Outreach

A study conducted by the Federal Trade Commission in September 2000 reported that adults are involved in the purchase of games 83% of the time,[7] so it is clear that parents are

6. The March 2008 results of this study show that 86% of parents are aware of the ratings and 78% use them regularly when choosing games for their families. Awareness of content descriptors is at 66% among the parents surveyed. Fifty-nine percent (59%) of those parents "never" allow their children to play M-rated games while 35% only do so "sometimes." These figures match very closely those reported by the FTC in 2007.
7. The FTC's more recent Report to Congress in 2007 found that parents are involved in the purchase of a video game 89% of the time.

either involved in or ultimately making the decision about what games their kids are playing an overwhelming majority of the time.

Keeping in mind the significant role parents play in making purchase decisions, the ESRB launched a multi-channel consumer marketing campaign in October 2003 featuring the slogan *"Ok To Play?—Check The Ratings."* The campaign, which is primarily composed of public service announcements and a retail partnership program, encourages parents to use both components of the rating system (rating symbols and content descriptors) to determine if a game is appropriate for their family.

The campaign generates over a billion consumer impressions annually. Over 20 publications have run the print PSA ads, and more than a dozen top game enthusiast publications support the campaign as well.

Because more than half of all games sold each year in the U.S. are sold during the holiday season, the ESRB also conducts an annual Holiday Outreach initiative that includes satellite television and radio media tours, print and radio PSAs, targeted outreach to parents through print and online outlets, and audio news releases. Last year's [2006] campaign generated approximately 150 million impressions during the holiday season alone.

Partnerships

Retail. A critical part of our consumer awareness campaign is its unique retail partnership program. The overall goal of our retailer partnerships is to ensure that consumers are educated about and reminded to check the ratings when they are shopping for computer and video games. Rather than send posters or stand-alone brochures to stores that consumers may not notice, we have succeeded in getting signage displayed in stores representing the 18 top national retail accounts representing 90% of game sales, many of which have incorporated ratings education into their in-store display fixtures. ESRB has also provided many of these retailers with materials for sales associates to learn about the rating system, and has facilitated the training of nearly 45,000 store associates through an online training module.

National PTA[8]

The ESRB has recently been working closely with the National PTA, whose president, Anna Weselak, called the ESRB ratings "an extremely useful and informative tool" while strongly encouraging parents to use it when choosing games for their families. ESRB is working with the NPTA to develop parent education materials that would be distributed to all state and local PTA chapters.

State and Local Governments[9]

ESRB has established partnerships with various state and local governments, working with leaders and officials to promote and educate parents about the ratings. County Executive Andy Spano (Westchester County, NY), Assemblyman Ed Chavez (D-CA), State Attorneys General Mark Shurtleff of Utah and Thurbert Baker of Georgia, Puerto Rico Secretary of Consumer Affairs Alejandro Garcia and others have teamed up with ESRB to implement PSA campaigns, educational brochures and other projects aimed at raising awareness and use of the ratings.

---

8. In 2006, ESRB and PTA developed and distributed over 1 million ratings education brochures to 26,000 PTAs nationwide. In 2008 this partnership was furthered through the distribution of "A Parent"s Guide to Video Games, Parental Controls and Online Safety," which was also distributed nationwide and was supplemented by a webcast featuring experts from ESRB, PTA, and GamerDad.com.

9. As of 2008, ESRB had teamed up on ratings education campaigns with Governors Ed Rendell of Pennsylvania and Christine Gregoire of Washington State, State Attorneys General Mark Shurtleff of Utah, Thurbert Baker of Georgia, Lawrence Wasden of Idaho, Patrick Lynch of Rhode Island, and Greg Abbott of Texas, as well as Delaware Lt. Gov. John Carney and State Representative Helene Keeley, Oklahoma State Senator Glenn Coffee, and County Prosecutor Carl Brizzi of Marion County, Indiana.

I *"The video game rating system ... has been confusing and contradictory, and the terms are not explicit enough to be taken literally."*

The Video Game Ratings System Is an Ineffective Regulation

Jonathan Harbour

Jonathan Harbour is senior instructor of game development at the University of Advancing Technology in Tempe, Arizona. In the following viewpoint, he argues that the Entertainment Software Rating Board (ESRB) ratings system is flawed. Harbour contends that there are too many ratings categories, and some seem to blur into each other. The inexactitude, he maintains, leaves most consumers confused. More disturbing, he notes, is that some games with adult content receive the more marketing-friendly "Mature" rating. This has added to parents' uncertainty concerning the inappropriate content to which their children are being exposed, Harbour states.

As you read, consider the following questions:

1. How do industry organizations like the IGDA (International Game Developers Association) defend violence in video games, much to Harbour's chagrin?

2. What critique does Harbour put forth about the ESRB's "E," "E10+," and "EC" ratings?

3. What types of adult content does Habour claim exist in "M" rated games?

Video game publishers are releasing games today that are filled with intense scenes of violence, sex, and profanity, and these games are being played by young children and teenagers in ever-growing numbers every day. Why is this a problem? Because video games are beginning to look more real today due to advanced 3D graphics technology. Thus, playing a realistic game is similar to a real-world situation.

That the U.S. Army is using first person shooters for recruitment and training is a telling point. The Interactive Digital Software Association (IDSA), a major trade association for the video game industry, succinctly describes the problem with the Entertainment Software Rating Board (ESRB) ratings system: "While the industry is making the same efforts to protect children it has over the past few years, research and anecdotal evidence show that the potential for harm from video games is much greater than previously understood. Increasing power (i.e. realism) of technology is one factor; our increased knowledge base is another. Despite some commitment to implementing our past recommendations, the industry is slipping backwards by standing still."

Game Developers Push the Limits of Acceptable Content

Studies have shown that there is a direct correlation between the consumption of violent media and aggressive behavior in children—and yet, industry-backed organizations such as the

International Game Developers Association (IGDA) deny such allegations and continue to praise the increasingly violent nature of games, citing freedom of expression and artistic license. The rating system currently in use is only partially effective at informing the consumer about the content of a video game, while publishers are continuing to push the limits of acceptable content to new levels each year (and thus, further negating the usefulness of prior ratings—which follows the IDSA statement above). I'm not concerned with debating one research study over another. Common sense dictates that children should not be exposed to scenes of violence, sexuality, or profanity. As far as I'm concerned, there is no relativistic debate over this issue. Anyone who exposes a child to such things should be treated in the same manner as those who commit child abuse—which can manifest itself in many forms.

There exists a serious gap in the marketplace for an intelligent, informative guide to the video game rating system. Why are the current ratings growing more ineffective each year? I believe violent video games are acceptable in the same context that violent movies are acceptable, when the rating system in use is effective at warning parents about the content. The video game rating system, ESRB, has described a rating system that, in the past, has been confusing and contradictory, and the terms are not explicit enough to be taken literally. As a result, ratings have not been used as intended by consumers. Most adults today grew up playing benign video games such as *Pac-Man* and *Donkey Kong*, while the games today are more accurately compared with films than their pixellated ancestors.

Ratings Confusion

I wish the ESRB would adopt a more aggressive stance on video game content, make recommendations for stronger enforcement of the ratings, and try to increase awareness of the existing system. Retailers should adopt a means for consumers

Video Games Cannot Be Described like Movies or Television Shows

The ESRB is . . . misguided in its steadfast attempts to rate video games just as if they were television or movies. Video games are simply a different medium. The strategy of rating 'content,' for example, while it works creakingly for more traditional media is not sufficient for video games. No matter how many content descriptors the ESRB comes up with, until they are able to give consumers a sense of things like the relative frequency or repetition of violence, whether violence is required in order to complete the game and whether violence is committed against the player, by the player or in non-interactive elements, the ratings system will always be lacking.

Aaron Ruby, "Is the ESRB Broken?"
Next Generation Web site,
October 2, 2006. www.next-gen.biz.

to better protect their children from inappropriate content. The desensitization of a child toward violence, sex, and profanity has an adverse affect on that child's development. In particular, several of the highest grossing games in video game history have focused on extreme violence against women, which is of particular concern to many parents. Decoding the video game ratings system is therefore a problem with many consumers. There are many games that have been inappropriately rated for their content. Here are the video game ratings today, established by the Entertainment Software Rating Board (ESRB):

- EC—Early Childhood: (Age 3+) Contains no inappropriate material.

- E—Everyone: (Age 6+) Minimal cartoon, fantasy, or mild violence and/or infrequent use of mild language.

- E10+—Everyone 10+: (Age 10+) More cartoon, fantasy, or mild violence, mild language and/or minimal suggestive themes.

- T—Teen: (Age 13+) May contain violence, suggestive themes, crude humor, minimal blood, simulated gambling, and/or frequent use of strong language.

- M—Mature 17+: (Age 17+) May contain intense violence, blood and gore, sexual content and/or strong language.

- AO—Adults Only 18+: (Age 18+) May include prolonged scenes of intense violence and/or graphic sexual content and nudity.

- RP—Rating Pending: Awaiting final rating.

This list of ratings now used to rate video games is confusing at best, and useless at worst. About the only thing concerned parents can do is limit their children's exposure to "E—Everyone" or "E10+—Everyone 10+", since games in these two categories, along with the obvious "EC—Early Childhood" are going to be very safe for children. However, why is there a need for three ratings in this category in the first place? The differences among them are negligible and simply add to the confusion. These three are equivalent to the movie industry's "G" rating. The "T—Teen" rating and "M—Mature 17+" rating are both abused by publishers, as far too many games are being released under the "T" rating when they belong in the "M" category. Likewise, you will find an occasional game rated "M" when it is clearly not offensive.

For an example of the inequality that leads to confusion, the game *Halo* is rated "M" while containing mild to moderate violence (against aliens, with purple blood). *Halo* is a science fiction game with a deep and complex storyline that plays out very much like a movie; however, instead of simply watching passively, viewers interact with the game world by assuming the identity of the protagonist—a Marine hero who is known only by his rank: Master Chief. There are many situations in this game where humans are killed, often brutally, but the violence is not seasoned with gore. There is none of the limb-severing effects found in movies like *Aliens* and *Starship Troopers.*

At the same time, *Grand Theft Auto: Vice City*, also rated "M", contains explicit scenes of violence against women, sexuality, prolific use of profanity, and illegal drugs, murder, and cop killing—all of which are part of the storyline in this game. Clearly, this game belongs in the "AO" category. There is a problem with the ratings system if two vastly different games (content-wise) are rated in same. It is analogous to rating the movies *Monsters, Inc.* and *Pulp Fiction* in the same category (such as PG) because *Monsters, Inc.* has fictionalized scary scenes. Does this make any logical sense? This is why consumers have been so confused about video game ratings, and why they have largely misunderstood the ratings—which renders them *useless. . . .*

While some parents may feel apathetic to exposing their children to violent content, it should be discouraged when possible. Video game publishers should discourage parents from buying adult-themed games (such as *Postal 2*) for children under the age of 18. Indeed, one clear flaw in the ESRB is declaring Mature for 17+, while Adult-Only is 18+. That makes no sense, and is directly responsible for most of the confusion on this matter. Mature games should not include any adult themes, but the lines are blurred. Any game that depicts violence against women, promotes drug use, encourages violence against police officers and other public servants (in particular, but also including violence against other humans or animals in general), uses vulgar profanity, or pornographic text (as in an adult book), should clearly be rated for Adult-

Only. But as was the case with the old X film rating, it attained an ego of its own, so that no game publisher will release an "AO" game due to the connotation that it contains pornography, even when the rating was not intended for that exclusive niche.

Unfortunately, the M(ature) rating has been grossly abused and for the most part, nearly every mildly-violent to very-violent game released now is rated M. That further degrades the usefulness of the ratings—in other words, there is no clear delineation between T(een) and M(ature) ratings, and most publishers lobby to keep their games below the AO rating, even when they belong there.

For the most part, parents care greatly about what their children are consuming in the media, and are very concerned about video game content. However, there has never been a thorough and effective guide written that clearly *shows what the ratings mean* and how a consumer *can use those ratings effectively*. Comparing video games to movies is a very useful method to compare how similar content should be graded on the ratings scale. While the video game industry has more ratings than the movie industry, it is actually a benefit, because the rating scale can be more informational to a consumer if understood. The ESRB ratings are insufficient because they are not effective. One obvious solution would be the adoption of the MPAA [Motion Picture Association of America] rating system. Unfortunately, those ratings are trademarks of the MPAA, and are therefore not usable unless game publishers join the MPAA. What the video game industry needs is the adoption of comparable ratings that parallel those in the movie industry to alleviate the confusion.

There is a lot of amazing talent in this industry, and there are many extraordinary games being made every year. What the game industry needs is not more congressional legislation and oversight, but rather, more self-governing, more responsibility, and more sensitivity to the public. To a certain degree, the game industry deserves criticism, for lack of effort in these areas (in fact, for maintaining a hard refusal to acknowledge that the problem even exists).

Periodical Bibliography

The following articles have been selected to supplement the diverse views presented in this chapter.

Education Week	"FCC Says TV Violence Could Be Regulated," May 2, 2007.
Richard Freed	"Pulling the Plug on Entertainment Industry Ratings," *Pediatrics*, June 2007.
Bill Gloede	"Big Brother Is Back," *Media Week*, May 21, 2007.
Katie Hafner	"U Is for Unheeded," *New York Times*, December 16, 2004.
Anita Hamilton, et al.	"Video Vigilantes," *Time*, January 10, 2005.
David Kushner	"Gaming's Worst Bully," *Rolling Stone*, November 16, 2006.
Stephen Labaton	"FCC Moves to Restrict TV Violence," *New York Times*, April 26, 2007.
Tara Parker-Pope	"Taking the Violence out of Videogames: What Parents Can Do before Kids Play," *Wall Street Journal*, August 9, 2005.
Joseph Pereira	"Games Get More Explicit—And So Do Warning Labels," *Wall Street Journal*, September 25, 2003.
Bart Peterson	"Protecting Our Children from Harmful Media Violence," *Nation's Cities Weekly*, October 29, 2007.
Ira Teinowitz	"Congress Mull Obscenity," *Television Week*, June 11, 2007.
Joelle Tessler	"Video Game Ratings: A Hot-Button Issue," *CQ Weekly*, August 14, 2006.

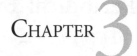

CHAPTER 3

What Are the Effects of Violence and Suffering in News Media Reporting?

Chapter Preface

Television news coverage is filled with images and reports of violent subject matter. From firefights in occupied Iraq to school shootings in the States, violence is often the focus of daily news hours, suggesting that such stories continually earn high audience ratings. For example, on April 16, 2007, when a gunman went on a murderous rampage that claimed the lives of thirty-two people at Virginia Tech in Blacksburg, Virginia, the story of the massacre and its aftermath accounted for just over half of the time devoted to news reporting from April 15 through April 20. That percentage dwarfed any other item in the country's news that week. Within two weeks, however, the story garnered only 1 percent of total news time, supporting the notion that programmers had already moved on to other items to capture fleeting audience interest.

Observers worry that the abundance of violent topics in television news reporting—and the intensity of coverage during each incident's peak period of interest—bolsters feelings of insecurity and aggression in viewers. In November 2002, the University of Missouri at Columbia released research by Tamyra Pierce concluding that the media's repetitive use of words such as "shoot," "kill," and "gun" might be triggering a receptive aggressive response in some television viewers. The study subjected 250 students (ages 18 to 25) to news programming that contained one report on a school shooting inserted among various nonviolent stories. According to the results, those students who had previously displayed depressive or insecure personality traits registered more aggressive thoughts when the violent news piece used the trigger words. As the university press release added, "The study also found that weapon words were the most severe trigger of aggressive thoughts and identification with perpetrators among insecurely attached and depressed individuals, but there was no difference in reactions between males and females."

Professor Pierce stated that the primary concern supported by such findings is that loners and social outcasts may be drawn to these stories and perhaps form an attachment to the perpetrators that would lead to copycat episodes. "The media used to publicize suicides, but now use extreme caution because of the number of copycat incidents that occurred as a result. However, they do not hesitate to give excessive coverage to shooting incidents," Pierce lamented. Whether aggressive news stories do incite copycat incidents is disputed, but as the viewpoints in the following chapter illustrate, many commentators share concerns that the barrage of news coverage involving episodes of real-world violence may be negatively impacting viewers by either triggering aggressive behavior or at least encouraging the notion that the world is largely malevolent and unsafe.

> *"For children, news can be a frightening thing, and with cable TV's 24-hour channels and the Internet, they are exposed to it more than ever before."*

Watching Violent News Has Harmful Effects on Children

Karen Goldberg Goff

In the following viewpoint, Karen Goldberg Goff examines the consequences America's addiction to cable TV's 24-hour news stations can have on our children. She turns to experts, such as John Murray, a professor of developmental psychology at Kansas State University who has spent 30 years studying TV violence and children. Murray reports that children can react in one of three ways to TV violence—they can become desensitized, fearful, or aggressive. Goff stresses that it is important to keep children informed, but that you can do that through newspapers or through discussions with your children rather than through the television, which can emphasize violence for the sake of ratings.

As you read, consider the following questions:

1. According to the author, how many hours per day does the typical American household have the television turned on?

Karen Goldberg Goff, "Restricting Reality; Parents Watching News on Television May be Giving their Children an Education in Subjects that Would be Rated R in Theaters," *Insight on the News*, June 3, 2002. Reproduced with permission of *Insight*.

2. How many students were killed in schools in the United States between 1999 and 2001, as cited in the viewpoint?

3. At what age does Joanne Cantor believe children are able to gain something valuable from watching the news?

For children, news can be a frightening thing, and with cable TV's 24-hour channels and the Internet, they are exposed to more of it than ever before. "I think we should let children know what is going on in the world but shield them from TV," says Joanne Cantor, professor emerita of communications at the University of Wisconsin.

Images on television can be much more upsetting than in the newspaper, says Cantor, author of *Mommy, I'm Scared: How TV and Movies Frighten Children and What We Can Do to Protect Them.* "TV news seeks viewers. To do that, it has to be dramatic and compelling, so producers are going to pick a higher rate of sensational news."

Bad News

Sensational or not, there is plenty of bad news these days. There also are plenty of televisions—65 percent of American children have one in their rooms, according to the American Academy of Pediatrics. Those televisions are on more than ever, too. John Murray, a professor of developmental psychology at Kansas State University, has spent 30 years studying TV violence and children. He says the typical American household has a television turned on seven hours a day.

"Both the local and national news give children the sense that the world is a dangerous place," Murray says. "Children begin to think there is not much you can do. You are born, you get shot, then you die."

On the other hand, children who view crime-related violence on television can become desensitized. It doesn't matter whether the violence is in a movie or on the 6 P.M. news report. "There are three effects of viewing TV violence," says Murray. "Children may become less sensitive to the pain and suffering of others. They may be more fearful of the world around them. Or they may be more likely to behave in aggressive or harmful ways toward others."

Monitoring or avoiding televisions and finding other sources for news are two ways parents can control the amount of scary imagery that gets into the house, says Miriam Baron, professor of pediatrics at Loyola University of Chicago. "There are some age-appropriate things parents can do without totally shielding their children," says Baron, chairwoman of the American Academy of Pediatrics' Public Education Committee. "To hear about some of the events in the world thirdhand can be just as scary." She advises parents to consider a child's developmental level if the television is going to be tuned to news. "I wouldn't let a 4-year-old watch it all," she says, "but at age 8 or 9, I would watch news with them and explain things."

TV News Is Not for Kids

Cantor agrees. "Really, children don't get anything valuable from watching the news until they are about 12," she says. "They are better off learning the news from their parents or by reading news magazines aimed at children." Paradoxically, older children may not be all that interested in the news. "It is usually the parents who have the news habit," says Cantor, adding that parents should, if possible, catch up on news in the evening rather than at the dinner hour when youngsters tend to be nearby. "But they should always be aware of what they are watching and what questions they are going to need to answer."

A news story doesn't have to show planes flying into buildings to scare youngsters. Stories about children can be terrify-

Rob Rogers: © The Pittsburgh Post-Gazette/Dist. By United Features Syndicate, Inc.

ing to other children. JonBenet Ramsey, the 6-year-old beauty queen found murdered in her Colorado home in 1996 is a good example.

"JonBenet never should have been a national story," Cantor says, "but when a really horrific thing happens, it becomes a national story. Then kids on the East Coast are worried about something that happened on the West Coast. The pictures bring it home. I got a call from a woman on the East Coast whose daughter was traumatized, who said she never wanted to be alone in the house again after watching a story on JonBenet on the Today show."

Younger children are more disturbed by coverage of natural disasters, however. Images often are dramatic—a home being ripped apart by a hurricane. These events are easy for children to understand and easily can cause them to develop fears.

Focus on the Positive

Rabbi Marc Gellman and Monsignor Thomas Hartman, coauthors of *Bad Stuff in the News: A Family Guide to Handling the Headlines*, lament that newscasters tend to focus on negative stories. The duo, who appear on TV talk shows as "The God Squad" to talk about the lessons of religion, ethics and values in everyday life, began their new book in the wake of the Columbine High School massacres. "What we are trying to say is that even with all the bad news, the situation is not helpless or hopeless," Hartman says. "With each bad thing they are likely to see on the news, there are things to understand."

In understanding a school shooting, for instance, it is important to remind children that fewer than 30 students were killed in schools in the United States between 1999 and 2001 and that millions go to schools every day and nothing bad ever happens to them. Being proactive can help young people feel they are doing their part to reduce evil in the world. If a child sees someone eating alone, he might ask him to have lunch once in a while, the authors say. "It may seem small, but asking a lonely kid to join you for lunch might be just the thing to convince that person that somebody cares about him or her. If he feels less lonely, he may feel less angry. If he feels less angry, he may have less pain inside. A simple act of kindness can go a long way."

"The era of school shooters was dawning, and it would clearly follow a copycat blueprint attentively 'followed,' if
not fueled, by the media."

Media Reports of Violent Crime Encourage Copycat Violent Acts

Loren Coleman

*Loren Coleman contends in the following viewpoint that school
shootings often share similar characteristics, which, he argues,
indicates that school shooters are spurred to imitative action following the news media's intense coverage of such incidents. Coleman, who began researching and consulting on copycat acts of
suicide and school shootings in the 1980s and currently operates
a blog with up-to-date information on current school shootings,
chronicles these events in the United States by observing trends
and patterns between different occurrences and noting the ways
in which the media participates by publicizing details. Further,
he offers suggestions to media outlets about how subsequent acts
could be discouraged in the future.*

As you read, consider the following questions:

1. What are the similarities among the several school shootings that Coleman observed prior to the Columbine school shooting?

2. According to Coleman, how did the September 11, 2001, terrorist attacks and the subsequent news coverage impact school shootings in the United States in the months following the attacks?

3. Why does Coleman suggest that the media avoid using cultural, ethnic, religious, or other stereotypes in portraying victims and perpetrators of school shootings?

Today's frenzied style of news coverage with its wall-to-wall "live news," "breaking news," and "continuing coverage" has become a modern form of entertainment. The newsroom's addiction for its own "reality programming" is a relatively recent phenomenon. It all began with CNN, the first news-only network on television, which has been around since 1980. Under Ted Turner's [owner and founder of the network] leadership, CNN was a groundbreaking idea, but it soon became "traditional" in terms of its low-impact, factual reportage of the news. By the mid-1990s, other news services began to promote an even more graphic "breaking news" style that led to today's MSNBC, Fox News, and other "news" networks. Fox News Network is a babe in these woods, evolving from the news department at Fox TV at the end of the 1996 elections. Everyone is now forced to compete for the latest breaking horror story. The modern world has given the media just what it wants most.

The News Media's Obsession Begins

Media interest in adolescent suicide clusters[1] reached a peak in 1987 with the Bergenfield incident [four teenagers killed themselves in a suicide pact by sitting in an idling car in a ga-

---

1. A phenomenon in which individuals from a specific population and location commit suicide in a similar way, often following an initial suicide by one individual.

rage]. Then through the early 1990s, stories about teen suicides faded from the national television, magazines, and newspapers. But it was just a matter of time before the media
would find a new, ever-more-sensational, *youth*-oriented death
phenomenon. And that would be school shootings.

The "modern era" [of] school rampages goes back to 1979
and Brenda Spencer, a 16-year-old girl, allegedly addicted to
violent films and killing birds with her bb gun. Her father had
given her a .22 semi-automatic for Christmas. Spencer would
later remark: "I ask him for a radio and he bought me a gun.
I felt like he wanted me to kill myself."

On January 29, 1979, Spencer pointed her gun out her
bedroom window to San Diego's Cleveland Elementary School
across the street. She waited for the principal to open the
school. At that point, Spencer began firing on the students
who were coming to school. For twenty minutes, she had the
students, teachers, and the crossing guard pinned down. During that period, Spencer killed the school principal and the
school's caretaker, as well as wounding nine students, aged 6
to 12. During the next two hours, Brenda Spencer talked to
the police and press, before finally surrendering. Explaining to
reporters what [she] had done, she said: "I just started shooting, that's it. I just did it for the fun of it. I just don't like
Mondays. . . . I just did it because it's a way to cheer the day
up. Nobody likes Mondays." She finally surrendered, and was
convicted on two counts of murder. Brenda Spencer is serving
two 25-to-life sentences. . . .

A decade would pass—almost to the day—before shootings at schools would start to be "news." On January 17, 1989,
Patrick Purdy, also known as Patrick West and by other names,
returned to the school he had attended 15 years before. But he
wasn't interested in a pleasant homecoming. Instead, Purdy,
wearing a t-shirt with the word Satan on it, opened fire at the
playground of the Cleveland Elementary School in Stockton,
California, killing 5 children and wounding 35 youngsters and

a teacher with his AK-47. All were the children of Southeast Asian refugees. Purdy then turned the gun on himself, and died by suicide.

Both the Purdy and Spencer incidents were atypical of the later school shooters pattern. Neither was [a] current member of the student body they attacked, and Spencer was female; most school shooters who caused fatalities in the late 1990s were males who were suicidal. But the era of school shooters was dawning, and it would clearly follow a copycat blueprint attentively "followed," if not fueled, by the media.

A New Blueprint

Although it attracted little attention by the media at the time, America's "first" modern school shooting took place on Groundhog's Day, February 2, 1996, at Moses Lake, Washington State. The Moses Lake killings set the pattern for what would follow in America—a student (not an outsider) killing other students and teachers. This is the horror—the danger from within of students killing students—that appears to have captivated the media. On that day, Barry Loukaitis, 14, dressed all in black, with boots and a long coat that hid his father's hunting rifle and two handguns, walked into his Frontier Junior High fifth-period algebra class at Moses Lake and started shooting. He had cut the pockets out of his long Western duster and was able to use the .30-.30 lever-action hunting rifle without taking his hands out of the long, black trench coat. Loukaitis killed two classmates (Arnold Fritz and Manuel Vela) and then severely wounded another (Natalie Hintz). Hintz, sitting beside the boys, was shot in the stomach, with the bullet traveling through her elbow and almost tearing her right arm off. Next, Loukaitis aimed at the back of his algebra teacher, Leona Caires, and killed her as she was writing an equation on the chalkboard. With the carnage around him and 15 students in the room crying hysterically, Loukaitis calmly turned toward them, smiled and said: "This sure beats algebra, doesn't it?" The line was a quote from the Stephen King novel, *Rage*. Physical education teacher Jon M. Lane then rushed into the room, knocked the rifle away from Loukaitis, and wrestled him to the floor to end the shooting. . . .

After the Loukaitis incident, the next "nationally publicized" shooting took place on February 19, 1997, at Bethel Regional High School in Bethel, Alaska, which had been a hotspot of suicide clusters a decade earlier. When student Evan Ramsey, 16, was feeling suicidal in 1997, he went to two 14-year-old friends and asked them what he should do. The boys said that if he was going to kill himself, he should take some people with him. On February 19, Ramsey did just that, killing a star athlete, Joshua Palacios, and wounding two others, with a 12-gauge shotgun. Then Ramsey went to the administration office and shot and killed the principal, Ronald Edwards. State police arrived and ended the rampage; they also arrested as accomplices the two friends who had discussed Ramsey's plan with him.

School Shootings Abound in Rural America

By the fall of 1997, school shooting would become horribly routine, almost as if some kind of copycat contagion was occurring. Of course, it was.

On October 1, 1997, in Pearl, Mississippi, Luke Woodham, 16, a self-styled Satanist and Adolf Hitler worshipper, stabbed his mother to death in the morning, and then drove to his Pearl High School. There he used a rifle to kill two students, former girlfriend Christina Menefee, 16, and Lydia Dew, 17, and to wound seven others. He only stopped because he ran out of ammunition. When he returned to his car for his other gun, the assistant principal disarmed him. . . .

Exactly two months later, on December 1, 1997, at Heath High School in West Paducah, Kentucky, Michael Carneal, 14, killed three students (Jessica James, 17, Kayce Steger, 15, and Nicole Hadley, 14) and wounded five as they participated in a prayer circle. Another student tackled the black-attired Carneal, and the police found that he had a pistol, two rifles, and two shotguns, along with 700 rounds of ammunition, all of it stolen. A copy of Stephen King's *Rage* was found in his locker at school.

On December 15, 1997, a similar scenario unfolded in Stamps, Arkansas. While hiding in the woods, Joseph "Colt" Todd, 14, shot two students as they stood in the parking lot. This appears to have been the direct model for the next shooting, also from Arkansas. On March 24, 1998, at Jonesboro, Arkansas, at the Westside Middle School, Mitchell Johnson, 13, and Andrew Golden, 11, both wearing camouflage, used rifles to shoot at their classmates and teachers from the woods. Four students (Natalie Brooks, 12, Paige Ann Herring, 12, Stephanie Johnson, 12, and Britthney Varner, 12) and one teacher (Shannon Wright, 32) were killed, while ten others were wounded outside as the school emptied during a false fire alarm set off by Golden. . . .

The imitation occurring in these copycat events was taking place both on the large scale and the small scale. On the macro level, the shootings were largely taking place in rural settings—in Washington State, Alaska, Mississippi, Kentucky, and Arkansas. And at the micro level, all involved suicidal-homicidal young males with guns. . . .

The Most Horrific School Shooting

Then the nightmare of April 1999 occurred.

On April 20, 1999, Eric Harris, 18, and Dylan Klebold, 17, killed 1 teacher and 12 students and wounded 23 others at Columbine High School in Littleton, Colorado. Focusing their attack on the cafeteria, Harris and Klebold spoke German and wore trench coats, as they reenacted scenes from *The Matrix* and *The Basketball Diaries* in the nation's deadliest school shooting. They had plotted for a year to kill at least 500 and blow up their school. At the end of their hour-long rampage, they turned their guns on themselves. . . .

In the wake of the shootings in Littleton, the nation's schools were under attack by copycats. Some 400 related incidents were reported in the month following the killings. "Across the nation after the 1999 Columbine tragedy," noted Court TV's Katherine Ramsland, "other kids called in bomb threats, wore trench coats to school, or used the Internet to praise what Klebold and Harris had done. Only ten days later, on April 30, people feared the eruption of some major event because that day marked Hitler's suicide in 1945. Schools in Arizona, New Jersey, Michigan, North Carolina, and D.C. closed to investigate potential threats. It wasn't Paducah, or Jonesboro, or Springfield that they wanted to imitate; the mantra was 'Columbine.'" . . .

Rethinking Policies to Stop School Shootings

School shootings continued in America after Columbine. The deaths by school shootings showed a gradual increase from 1996 to 1999, and then a sudden jump. In the post-Columbine era, school and city officials realized for the first time that dealing with at-risk youth—whether suicidal, angry, or impulsive—might prevent more school shootings. After Columbine, the United States Secret Service studied school shootings, and in March 2001, declared that zero tolerance punishments, such as expelling students who wore trench coats, was the wrong approach. That simply sent the youths out of schools, only to return later with guns and cause a rampage. The U.S. Secret Service study mentioned that a majority of the student shooters were suicidal and knew about previous shootings.

Youth advocates began to discuss the excessive, and often irresponsible, coverage of school shootings. Center on Juvenile and Criminal Justice president Vincent Schiraldi told Youth Beat reporters LynNell Hancock and Donna Ladd in 2002 that the media are creating youth-violence connections where they do not exist and giving the public a distorted picture of young people in America. "The media really have no clue as to how to deal with this at this point. And I'm not sure many in the media are concerned," he said about the "wall-to-wall coverage" of the school shootings. "What's the plan here, guys?"

The Positive Effects of Terrorism on School Shootings

Suicide prevention training increased, but the copycat factor received little attention. Before September 11, 2001, media attention seemed focused on what school shooting might be next. When the terrorist attack occurred, a virtual media blackout kept other violence out of the news. But, in fact, there were no shooting rampages in American schools during the entire scholastic year 2001–2002. Little did the media notice or comment on the fact that school shootings had decreased so precipitously when they weren't reporting on them. . . .

For a while in the wake of the terrorist events of September 11, 2001, when a virtual media moratorium occurred with regard to reporting school shootings and workplace rampages because the mass media concentrated mostly on terrorism and war, the number of copycat incidents of these kinds of rampage shootings dropped to almost zero in the United States. By 2003, however, the media had returned to reporting sensational stories of local violence, again feeding the copycat effect frenzies of the recent past.

Media Responsibility

Suicides, murder-suicides, and murders—the events that are at the core of the most negative projections of the copycat effect—will remain newsworthy in the eyes of the media in the foreseeable future and will continue to be reported. So what, short of self-censorship, should the media do to halt the contagion of the copycat effect? While the recommendations of

News Coverage of Suicide Increases Copycat Suicides

Since 1990, the effect of media coverage on suicide rates has been documented in many other countries besides the United States, ranging from Western countries including Austria, Germany, and Hungary to Australia and to East Asian countries, such as Japan. This has added to the extensive work prior to 1990 in the United States, which found considerable evidence that suicide stories in the mass media, including newspaper articles and television news reports . . . are followed by a significant increase in the number of suicides.

The magnitude of the increase in suicides following a suicide story is proportional to the amount, duration, and prominence of media coverage. . . . In a quantitative analysis of 293 findings from 42 studies, [Wayne State University researcher Steven] Stack (2000) found that studies assessing the effect of the suicide of an entertainer or political celebrity were 14.3 times more likely to find a "copycat" effect than studies that did not. Furthermore, studies based on real suicides in contrast to fictional stories were 4.03 times more likely to find an imitation effect. Although Stack did not identify any age-specific effects, the impact of suicide stories on subsequent completed suicides has been reported to be greatest for teenagers.

Madelyn Gould, Patrick Jamieson, and Daniel Romer,
American Behavioral Scientist, *May 2003.*

prevention experts during the last two decades have applied specifically to suicides, I have generalized them so that they also apply to all forms of violence that fall under the media-driven propagation of the copycat effect.

Here then are my seven recommendations:

1. The media must be more aware of the power of their words. Using words like "successful" sniper attacks, suicides, and bridge jumpers, and "failed" murder-suicides, for example, clearly suggests to viewers and readers that someone should keep trying again until they "succeed." We may wish to "succeed" in relationships, sports, and jobs, but we do not want rampage or serial killers, architects of murder-suicide, and suicide bombers to make further attempts after "failing." Words are important. Even the use of "suicide" or "rampage" in headlines, news alerts, and breaking bulletins should be reconsidered.

2. The media must drop their clichéd stories about the "nice boy next door" or the "lone nut." The copycat violent individual is neither mysterious nor healthy, or usually an overachiever. They are often a fatal combination of despondency, depression, and mental illness. School shooters are suicidal youth that slipped through the cracks, but it is a complex issue, nevertheless. People are not simple. The formulaic stories are too often too simplistic.

3. The media must cease its graphic and sensationalized wall-to-wall commentary and coverage of violent acts and the details of the actual methods and places where they occur. Photographs of murder victims, tapes of people jumping off bridges, and live shots of things like car chases ending in deadly crashes, for example, merely glamorize these deaths, and create models for others—down to the method, the place, the timing, and the type of individual involved. Even fictional entertainment, such as the screening of *The Deer Hunter*, provides vivid copycatting stimuli for vulnerable, unstable, angry, and depressed individuals.

4. The media should show more details about the grief of the survivors and victims (without glorifying the death), highlight the alternatives to the violent acts, and mention the relevant background traits that may have brought this event to this deathly end. They should also avoid setting up the incident as a logical or reasonable way to solve a problem.

5. The media must avoid ethnic, racial, religious, and cultural stereotypes in portraying the victims or the perpetrators. Why set up situations that like-minded individuals (e.g. neo-Nazis) can use as a roadmap for future rampages against similar victims?

6. The media should never publish a report on suicide or murder-suicide without adding the protective factors, such as the contact information for hot lines, help lines, soft lines, and other available community resources, including e-mail addresses, Web sites, and phone numbers. To run a story on suicide or a gangland murder without thinking about the damage the story can do is simply not responsible. It's like giving a child a loaded gun. The media should try to balance such stories with some concern and consideration for those who may use it to imitate the act described.

7. And finally, the media should reflect more on their role in creating our increasingly violent society. Honest reporting on the positive nature of being alive in the 21st century might actually decrease the negative outcomes of the copycat effect, and create a wave of self-awareness that this life is rather good after all. Most of our lives are mundane, safe, and uneventful. This is something that an alien watching television news from outer space, as they say, would never know. The media should "get real," and try to use their influence and the copycat effect to spread a little peace, rather than mayhem.

"The media do not cover progress nearly as well as they cover tragedy, scandal, and decay."

News Media Should Provide a Context for the Violence They Report

Mortimer B. Zuckerman

Mortimer B. Zuckerman, editor in chief for U.S. News and World Report, *writes in the following viewpoint that U.S. television news has skewed the American public's perception of the positive progress being made in the Iraq War. He further argues that U.S. policy makers have based many of their decisions about how to proceed in the war on this perception, even though it was created erroneously through misinformation and an overwhelming focus on negative events. Zuckerman calls for all news organizations and reporters to think critically about the potential impact of reporting on violence and to provide context that will place horrors within a larger understanding of events.*

As you read, consider the following questions:

1. What did Warren Christopher mean when he said that television cannot be "the North Star of America's foreign policy"?

2. According to Zuckerman, what has exacerbated the problem of media confusing, rather than enlightening, their audiences?

3. What does Zuckerman suggest individuals involved in the media do to reduce the negative impact of their reporting?

The city is ablaze, the bodies dismembered. This time it's Beirut, and the pictures are as horrific as those from Baghdad, Madrid, and Jerusalem. Cowardly atrocities are calculated to kill but, even more, to affect public opinion. Take Iraq. On the scale of warfare, the number of casualties in Iraq is relatively few. Every single one is a tragedy, but the images repeated over and over again on TV can drive government agendas and policy decisions. When we see American soldiers blown up night after night on the news, the images lead many of us to conclude that the Iraq war was a political miscalculation and a military disaster. How can America conduct foreign policy when that policy is perceived by policy makers and the public through the distorted lens of TV? Television, as former Secretary of State Warren Christopher once said, simply cannot be the North Star of America's foreign policy.

In Iraq, the suicide attacks on our soldiers are clearly meant to dishearten us all. The proof that the assassins have an eye on the media impact as much as on their murders and hostage-takings is that they dramatize them with videos of decapitations they expect to be endlessly recycled. In this, alas, they are not disappointed.

An Overwhelming Focus on the Negative

The result? Too often, policy making is held hostage to imagery. TV networks, especially cable, have neither the time nor the resources to convey memory or history, and thus they distort the meaning of events by failing to provide the context that would help us make sense of these images.

The media do not cover progress nearly as well as they cover tragedy, scandal, and decay. "If it bleeds, it leads" is a time-worn TV newsroom cliché. One car bomb wreaking destruction amid smoking Iraqi buildings is more likely to be aired than images of 100 rebuilt schools. A handful of bad guys with video cameras can prove more powerful than a platoon of engineers fixing sewers. And so, bad news drives out good. A premium is placed on finding out what's wrong as opposed to telling the full story of what's going right and wrong. Every policy will have some flaws and thus provide opportunities for the media to focus on what went wrong. But in an age of instant mass media, it is imperative not to define every major policy or decision or military operation on the basis of its inevitable flaws: Yes, the Iraqi election did not solve all the problems; yes, it was only a beginning, but good heavens, what a beginning!

Doing a Disservice to the Public and U.S. Leaders

At a time when modern TV journalism demands action images and boffo pictures, our leaders are going to have to find ways to provide TV images that will dramatize their policies if they hope to have adequate public support. In Iraq, for example, the government might well have helped the media focus, especially with pictures, on the grisly new evidence of the crimes against humanity committed during Saddam Hussein's reign of terror.

The tendency for the electronic media to confuse rather than enlighten is exacerbated by the fact that TV talk shows have more and more fused with news so that assertions now regularly masquerade as fact. The same is true of blogging. Opinion congeals miraculously into conviction when audiences follow segmented media that reinforce what they already believe. Public discourse thus veers toward oversimplification and hype as network news-gathering declines and foreign bureaus close.

Media Complicity in Propagating Messages of Terror

While the use of violence (individual or group) is *the* hallmark of terror (especially indiscriminate killing), users of such vile means cannot be satisfied with killing per se. It is not (only) the rhetoric of justice terrorists are after, but the rhetoric of justification. They desire that their use of lethal power be explained, justified, and accepted as *legitimate* not only by themselves but by sympathetic others. The media enter the equation at exactly this point. In the distant past, with the limited distribution of the media (mostly newspapers), achieving such an effect was much more difficult. With the ubiquity of electronic and printed mass media in the second half of the 20th century, using the media to persuade spectators of the appropriateness of any specific struggle has become part and parcel of the conduct of different (not all) groups who use terror. In fact, some of these groups even use sympathetic graduates of communication programs as advisors.

For media representations of terror to achieve an effect of persuasion, they need to appear as 'morally right.' Legitimization of a struggle of any group (or state) that uses terror requires that moral boundaries be redrawn. . . .

Nachman Ben-Yehuda,
International Journal of Comparative Sociology, *2005.*

The public, obviously, is ill-served by all this, but so are our leaders. In an increasingly partisan nation, a leader can convince one half, but not the other, leaving us without a democratic consensus, vulnerable to divisive actions by our enemies. What's to be done? Recognizing the problem is a start. Government might well have to imagine media scenarios and plan for them, just as they plan for battlefield options.

A Call for Self-Discipline

Television executives and on-air talent, too, should pause to consider their role in all this. This is not to suggest censorship so much as self-discipline and respect for complexity: Journalism with context is vastly more valuable than Journalism without. It is a service neither to journalism nor to the public to romanticize gore and violence and corrupt our public discourse by the distortion of language. Murders of innocent hostages are not "executions," with the false implication of due process. They are murders. The terrorist is not a commando or a guerrilla, and the spiritual leader who incites or condones killings is no such thing. The term is a disgraceful oxymoron.

The media have practiced self-discipline in relation to pornography without violating the canons of good journalism. It is no violation of either journalism or good judgment to remember that there is no moral neutrality between terrorists and the people and societies they attack.

"The scariest thing, after all, is not spy thrillers; it's that our leaders adopt their rhetoric."

Violence in Television Shows Mirrors Violence from the News

Clive Thompson

In the following viewpoint, Clive Thompson examines the ways in which fictional television portrayals of violence often mirror, and sometimes predict, real-life events. When onscreen violence reflects real life, Thompson hopes that a meaningful debate can ensue—one in which Americans can discuss why both real and fictional violence maintain their continuing attraction. What Thompson fears, however, is when America's leaders begin to mold their behavior on or seek justification for their violent policies in the fictional heroics of television characters. Thompson writes about science, technology, and culture and contributes regularly to New York Times Magazine, Wired, Fast Company, Discover, *and* New York *magazine.*

Clive Thompson, "Cruel Intentions," *New York*, January 31, 2005. Reproduced with the permission of *New York* Magazine.

As you read, consider the following questions:

1. What are some of the specific correlations Clive Thompson makes between fictional violence in television shows and instances of violence in the news?

2. How does Bob Cochran, the creator of the television series *24*, justify the torture scenes in his television show?

3. What does Thompson view as the "scariest thing" about television shows' depictions of violence, and what does he argue to be the value in these shows?

In the season opener of the spy show *Alias*, the heroine, Sydney Bristow, was captured and, in the delicate argot of espionage, "interrogated." The villain shackled her to a chair, strapped a gas mask on her face, and hooked it up to a hose. Then he filled the mask with water—drowning her on dry land as she writhed helplessly.

It was a chilling scene, and not simply because of the violence itself. I realized I was watching a variant of "waterboarding," the near-drowning torture the CIA has reportedly used on suspected terrorist detainees. I'd read about it in coverage of the Guantánamo hearings that very same morning. And that was hardly the first time a spy show had mimicked a real-life scandal. For the past three years, shows like *Alias*, *24*, and *MI-5* have provided a perverse mirror of the real-life response to terror: They've reflected, and sometimes eerily predicted, the rise of torture as a government policy.

Torture Shows

Some of this is mere coincidence; stylized violence is the vocabulary of pop culture, and thrillers have always included torture in the mix: We have ways of making you talk, Mr. Bond. Still, the sheer preponderance of torture scenes on TV right now is unusual, and this crop of smart thrillers—of which I'm a big fan—began twisting the thumbscrews right after 9/11, three years before Guantánamo and Abu Ghraib hit the headlines. *Alias* launched nineteen days after the World Trade Center attacks, and the premiere episode included a scene where a torturer ripped out the heroine's back teeth. The shows are unusually good at capturing the dark sensuality of torture: the Cartesian horror of being trapped in a vulnerable body, the sub-dom relationship of the torturer and his victim.

Most often in these shows it's the villains being villainous, but regularly—and more interestingly—it's the good guys in the tormentor's seat. Sometimes they're state agents desperate to coax out bomb codes; sometimes they're CIA agents seeking revenge. In *24*, the dark hero, Jack Bauer, has shot a suspect in the leg, squeezed bullet wounds, and withheld a bottle of heart-attack medicine. In *Alias*, the heroine is ethically pristine—she never tortures—but other CIA agents do. At the end of last season, Sydney's love interest Vaughn discovered his wife was a double agent; he strung her up by her arms and pulled out the inevitable creepy bag of brushed-chrome surgical tools. It's moments like this where the shows seem most directly to channel the political question of our time: What does it mean when our government resorts to torture?

Art Predicting Real Life

Sometimes, the answer's simple: It debases us. For sheer Cassandra-like precision, you can't beat Tom Fontana's movie *Strip Search*, which first aired on HBO last spring. It depicted a female U.S. interrogator sexually taunting an Arab detainee, a scenario that critics denounced as "silly and specious"— until a week later, when the Abu Ghraib abuses were exposed. According to Fontana, *Strip Search* was inspired by a direct reading of the Patriot Act in early 2002. As the creator of *Oz* and *Homicide: Life on the Street*, he knew the rules of interrogation, and he could see that they had moved the line. He was deeply troubled when the real-life abuses came forward. "You

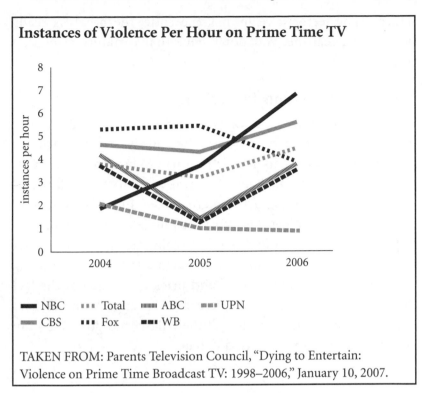

Instances of Violence Per Hour on Prime Time TV

Legend: NBC, Total, ABC, UPN, CBS, Fox, WB

TAKEN FROM: Parents Television Council, "Dying to Entertain: Violence on Prime Time Broadcast TV: 1998–2006," January 10, 2007.

know what? I wish I had made it all up. I wish I had made it up in my twisted imagination, and that the world hadn't caught up with me."

I've wondered whether these shows treat suffering as entertainment or, worse, make government torturers seem heroic. Bauer may be a grim figure, but he's portrayed with the sort of no-nonsense, take-charge style that Republicans revere. And with Abu Ghraib, many Americans simply snickered at the revelations; the very fact that the soldiers were cheerily e-mailing thumbs-up photos to friends back home indicated that they simply didn't think this would bother anybody. But Bob Cochran, the co-creator of *24*, argues that the torture in *24* doesn't have that effect, and that the role of the show is to explore these debates. Even when his government characters inflict pain, they're doing it in theoretically "ideal" circumstances: The terrorist really has the code, the bomb is really ticking. "In real life, you don't have that certainty," Cochran adds.

Not a Reaffirmation for Torture

The truth is, there's no way to simply praise or denounce these scenes. The scariest thing, after all, is not spy thrillers; it's that our leaders adopt their rhetoric. When I watched Sydney Bristow tortured, I knew it was a schlocky Hollywood ploy, a way of making a premiere racier. But it was also an imaginative leap. When her mask fills up with water, you have to think about what waterboarding really means. We shouldn't look to art as a guidepost for behavior. It's more confusing than that: at once numbing us and pricking at us. But the fact that such shows cater to our creepier revenge fantasies isn't reason to condemn them; for all their flash and gore, they can also be a step toward a moral debate.

Periodical Bibliography

The following articles have been selected to supplement the diverse views presented in this chapter.

Pauline W. Chen
"Another Day, Another Kidnapping," *Wilson Quarterly*, Summer 2007.

Joan Deppa
"Coping With a Killer's 'Manifesto,'" *Chronicle of Higher Education*, May 11, 2007.

Donna Freydkin
"New Reality: Right Up Close with the Gore," *USA Today*, November 14, 2002.

Kristin A. Goss
"Good Policy, Not Stories, Can Reduce Violence," *Chronicle of Higher Education*, May 4, 2007.

Dan Kennedy
"The Daniel Pearl Video," *Nieman Reports*, Fall 2002.

Diane E. Levin
"When the World Is a Dangerous Place," *Educational Leadership*, April 2003.

Roy Malone
"Online Harassment: A Hoax, A Suicide—A Journalistic Dilemma," *St. Louis Journalism Review*, December 2007.

Sean McCleneghan
"'Reality Violence' on TV News: It Began with Vietnam," *Social Science Journal*, 39.4, 2002.

Jeff J. McIntyre
"Media Violence in the News," *American Behavioral Scientist*, August 2003.

Neil Munro
"The Dollar Value of Murder," *National Journal*, February 17, 2007.

Emma Rosenblum
"Bad 'Vice'? Bohemian Tragedy," *New York*, April 30, 2007.

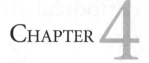

CHAPTER 4

Is the Internet a New Medium for Violence?

Chapter Preface

In a 2004 article in *Reader's Digest*, Michael Crowley noted disturbing similarities between the deaths of *Wall Street Journal* reporter Daniel Pearl and American businessman Nick Berg. Both men were Jewish and had been abducted by Islamic radicals, Crowley notes, and both had their subsequent executions videotaped and displayed on the Internet. What upsets Crowley most, however, is that it was not solely Islamic militant Web sites making these murderous videos available; American-run sites were advertising the tragic images for download to their clientele. According to Crowley, one U.S. Web site bearing the motto "Can You Handle Life?" "displays hundreds of images of dead, dying and mangled human beings. Some of its recent offerings were listed under titles such as 'shocking murder images,' 'suicide by grenade' and 'people who drowned.'"

Crowley contends that the Internet has plenty of venues for the curious to peruse photos and videos of car accident victims, gangland slayings, and celebrity corpses, as well as live-action shootings, burnings, beatings, explosions, and other tragedies. Comparing it to the plethora of sexually explicit videos and imagery that pervades the Internet, Crowley calls the morbid offerings "violence porn"—"the latest degradation of our popular culture, in which gruesome injuries and deaths are glorified and presented in wincing detail." He further claims that such sites are extremely popular, some receiving more than 150,000 visitors each day and earning their operators hefty sums from advertisers and subscription fees.

While many of the subscription sites can shield themselves by asserting that these violent videos are not available to casual visitors, other sites offer up images for free. This has invoked the ire of parents and teachers who find that children routinely drop in to check out the latest horror. And because more commonly visited forums such as YouTube.com and MySpace.com are screened for videos that portray death or serious injury, young viewers have moved on to other sites where everything from outright brutality to injurious pranks are cataloged for download. As Bob Sullivan, writing for MSNBC.com, reports, some of these sites even hand out monetary awards for outrageous videos in which poorly executed stunts or miscalculated pranks result in injury. Sullivan notes that viewer polls choose the winners, suggesting that anyone can witness the violent tapes and vote for his or her favorite. He further comments that the prize money ensures a flood of copycat videos in which participants try to mirror the episode in hopes of achieving a bit of fame.

In the following chapter, various observers and analysts discuss whether the Internet has become the newest forum for media violence. According to many reviewers, the Internet's ability to mask identity has made it a unique means of posting and viewing violent material. Furthermore, this anonymity has made it a preferred venue for perpetrating threats of violence. Many champion the lack of regulation that keeps the Internet a free and diverse medium, but to those like Michael Crowley, the unfettered display of wanton violence is "a warning that we're neck-deep in slime, and sinking fast."

> *"Although [cyber-bullying] is less physical than traditional forms of bullying, it can have more devastating and longer-lasting effects."*

Cyber-Bullying Is Worse than Physical Bullying

Scott Meech

In the following viewpoint, Scott Meech discusses the rise of cyber-bullying, schoolchildren's use of the Internet or cell phones to intimidate their peers. Meech claims that cyber-bullying is widespread in America. He also asserts that this form of harassment is worse than physical bullying because it subjects the victim to humiliation from a large audience, since embarrassing pictures or taunts are typically spread throughout a peer group. Furthermore, Meech states that victims have no safe haven from cyber-bullying because it reaches into homes and invades the technologies most children now depend upon for communication. Scott Meech is a computer and technology teacher at the Plano Middle School in Illinois.

As you read, consider the following questions:

1. According to the author, how do Paris and Robert Strom define cyber-bullying? How does Meech wish to amend their definition?

2. Why is cyber-bullying a difficult problem for authorities to handle, in Meech's view?

3. What two pieces of advice does Meech give to protect oneself from cyber-bullying?

To most teachers, the general stereotype of a bully is an over-sized male student who uses verbal and/or physical abuse to torment the smaller or weaker child. This stereotype is perpetuated throughout pop culture.

But the Internet has changed that, as it has changed so much else. Now there is "Cyber Bullying," and although it is less physical than traditional forms of bullying, it can have more devastating and longer-lasting effects. It is rapidly becoming a major problem. Now, a small physically weak child can be as much of a bully as the big brute but with more impact. Educators definitely need to understand how powerful and dangerous this new type of bullying has become as it has greatly impacted the classroom.

[Education professors] Paris and Robert Strom define cyber bullying as harassment using an electronic medium (e-mail, chat rooms, cell phones, instant messaging, and online voting booths) to threaten or harm others. This author believes that the definition should also include any form of information posted on the Internet, as in blogs, forums, etc. This latter form of cyber bullying involves gossip, humiliation, and threats.

Many Children Are Victims

The statistics are shocking. In the year 2000 a University of New Hampshire study found that one out of every 17, or 6 percent of kids in the United States, had been threatened or harassed online. But in March of 2006, statistics showed that 75 to 80 percent of 12 to 14 year olds had been cyber bullied. Furthermore, 20 percent of kids under 18 have received a sexual solicitation. So cyber bullying is clearly on the rise, and it affects both genders. An American Educational Research Association study [from 2006] shows that female bullies preferred the use of text messaging harassment versus face-to-face bullying by 2 to 1.

Cyber bullying is a very difficult form of bullying to prevent and to police. A major difference between cyber bullying and traditional bullying is the ability to bully without a face-to-face confrontation. Kids become emboldened by the false feeling of being anonymous and they say things they might not have said in person. Unfortunately, identifying a cyber bully isn't as easy as identifying the traditional big bad bully.

Authorities have greater difficulty in tracking down the bully because of problems in identification. Students are too often lax in their security with usernames and passwords so messages can be falsely written by individuals and misrepresented.

No Refuge from Harassment

The long-term impact of cyber bullying is greater than with traditional bullying. Digital images, cell phones, and other electronic means can greatly increase the speed in which the bully's messages can spread. Strom and Strom write, "Harmful messages intended to undermine the reputation of a victim can be far more damaging than face-to-face altercations. Instead of remaining a private matter or event known by only a small group, text or photographs can be communicated to a large audience in a short time."

Perhaps the greatest long-term effect is the loss of the home as a safe-zone. Traditional bullying usually ended when a person was home, safe with his or her family. Cyber bullying enters into the home and is with the students at all times. As

A Problem Still in Its Infancy

Research into the causes and effects of cyber-bullying is still in its infancy. But it is becoming clear that aspects of online communication encourage people to act aggressively, prompting them to do things they wouldn't dare to try in real life.

What's more, the ability to reach more people, and the always-on culture of the Internet, means that cyber-bullying can have an even more detrimental effect on the victim than conventional playground bullying. "It's school-yard bullying taken to the next level," says Justin Patchin, a criminologist at the University of Wisconsin, Eau Claire. A study by UK-based internet market research firm YouGov in 2006 found that for 1 in 8 young people cyber-bullying is even worse than physical bullying.

Phil McKenna, New Scientist, *July 21, 2007.*

[*USA Today* reporter] Greg Toppo writes, "Vulnerable children have virtually no refuge from harassment. It's a non-stop type of harassment and it creates a sense of helplessness." Bullies use this additional terror to traumatize their victims even more.

Our youth have grown up with technology; to them it is commonplace and part of their everyday life. Taking technology away from kids to protect them is not the answer, as they have integrated its use to such an extent that it would now begin to isolate them within their peer circles. Besides, the technology in itself is not bad; it is the manner in which it is used.

Educating Children About Cyber-Bullying

Students need to be educated on how to deal with cyber bullying as much as learning the traditional issues of drugs, sex, and nutrition. There are additional strategies that should be employed when dealing with cyber bullying. Never respond to a cyber bully. This just provides fodder and they now know that have actually made official contact. Protect your personal information with technology and change your online information including password and screen names on a regular basis.

Technology is changing the world in many ways. However, new negative uses of it have increased as well. Cyber bullying is on the rise and it is very serious.

| "Overall, both boys and girls say that kids their age are more likely to be harassed offline."

Cyberbullying Is Not Worse than Physical Bullying

Amanda Lenhart

Amanda Lenhart is a senior research specialist at the Pew Internet & American Life Project, a nonprofit organization that researches the impact of the Internet on American society and culture. She reports in the following viewpoint that cyber-bullying, the harassment of people over the Internet, cell phones, or other novel communications media, is a problem in the computer age. Lenhart states that cyber-bullying is most common among young people and that about a third of teenagers polled by Pew in 2006 reported being the victim of this form of intimidation. Most of these teens said they had private e-mails or other messages publicly disclosed. However, Lenhart asserts that the respondents to the Pew survey claimed that traditional bullying was still more common than online harassment.

As you read, consider the following questions:

1. What percentage of teens in the Pew survey said that bullying was more likely to occur off-line than online?

Amanda Lenhart, "Cyberbullying and Online Teens," *Pew Internet & American Life Project*, June 27, 2007. www.pewinternet.org. Reproduced by permission.

2. According to Lenhart, are girls or boys more likely to be the victims of the online rumor mill?

3. As Lenhart relates, what percentage of online teens who do not use social networking sites report having embarrassing photos posted on the Internet?

About one third (32%) of all teenagers who use the Internet say they have been targets of a range of annoying and potentially menacing online activities—such as receiving threatening messages; having their private e-mails or text messages forwarded without consent; having an embarrassing picture posted without permission; or having rumors about them spread online.

Depending on the circumstances, these harassing or "cyberbullying" behaviors may be truly threatening, merely annoying or relatively benign. But several patterns are clear: girls are more likely than boys to be targets; and teens who share their identities and thoughts online are more likely to be targets than are those who lead less active online lives.

Of all the online harassment asked about, the greatest number of teens told us that they had had a private communication forwarded or publicly posted without their permission. One in 6 teens (15%) told us someone had forwarded or posted communication they assumed was private. About 13% of teens told us that someone had spread a rumor about them online, and another 13% said that someone had sent them a threatening or aggressive e-mail, IM or text message. Some 6% of online teens told us that someone had posted an embarrassing picture of them without their permission.

Yet when asked where they thought bullying happened most often to teens their age, the majority of teens, 67%, said that bullying and harassment happens more *offline* than online. Less than one in three teens (29%) said that they thought that bullying was more likely to happen online, and 3% said they thought it happened both online and offline equally.

These results come from a nationally-representative phone survey of 935 teenagers by the Pew Internet & American Life Project. . . .

Victims of the Rumor Mill

Girls are more likely than boys to say that they have ever experienced cyberbullying—38% of online girls report being bullied, compared with 26% of online boys. Older girls in particular are more likely to report being bullied than any other age and gender group, with 41% of online girls ages 15 to 17 reporting these experiences. Teens who use social network sites like MySpace and Facebook and teens who use the Internet daily are also more likely to say that they have been cyberbullied. Nearly 4 in 10 social network users (39%) have been cyberbullied in someway, compared with 22% of online teens who do not use social networks.

The most commonly experienced bullying is having someone take a private e-mail, IM or text message and forwarding it on to someone else or posting the communication publicly. Nearly 1 in 6 (15%) of online teens said they had experienced unwanted forwarding of private communication. Older teens (ages 15–17) say they are more likely to have had someone forward or publicly post private messages—18% of older teens have experienced this, compared with 11% of younger teens.

A bit more than one in eight or 13% of teens said that someone had spread a rumor about them online. A girl in middle school told us: "I know a lot of times online someone will say something about one person and it'll spread and then the next day in school, I know there's like one of my friends, something happened online and people started saying she said something that she never said, and the next day we came into school and no one would talk to her and everyone's ignoring her. And she had no idea what was going on. Then someone sent her the whole conversation between these two people."

Making Private Information Public Is the Most Common Form of Cyberbullying		
Have you, personally, ever experienced any of the following things online?		
	Yes	No
Someone taking a private email, IM, or text message you sent them and forwarding it to someone else or posting it where others could see it	15%	85%
Someone spreading a rumor about you online	13%	87%
Someone sending you a threatening or aggressive email, IM, or text message	13%	87%
Someone posting an embarrassing picture of you online without your permission	6%	94%
Answer "yes" to any of the four previous questions	32%	68%

TAKEN FROM: Pew Internet & American Life Project Parents and Teens Survey, October–November, 2006.

Girls are more likely to report someone spreading rumors about them than boys, with 16% of girls reporting rumor-spreading compared with 9% of boys. Social network users are more likely than those who do not use social networks to report that someone had spread a rumor about them (16% vs. 8%).

Threats and Embarrassing Photos

One in eight online teens (13%) reported that someone had sent them a threatening or aggressive e-mail, instant message or text message. One fifteen-year-old boy in a focus group admitted, "I played a prank on someone but it wasn't serious . . . I told them I was going to come take them from their house and kill them and throw them in the woods. It's the best prank because it's like 'oh my god, I'm calling the police' and I was like 'I'm just kidding, I was just messing with you.' She got so scared though."

Older teens, particularly 15- to 17-year-old girls, are more likely to report that they have received a threatening e-mail or message. Overall, 9% of online teens ages 12–14 say they have been threatened via e-mail, IM or text, while 16% of online teens ages 15–17 report similar harassment. . . .

Fewer teens, some 6%, reported that someone had posted an embarrassing picture of them online without their permission. Not surprisingly, given the number of photos posted on social networking Web sites, users of those sites are more likely to report that someone had posted embarrassing pictures of them online without their permission—9% of social network users reported this, compared with just 2% of those who do not use social networking sites. Similarly, teens who post photos themselves are more likely to report that someone has posted an embarrassing photo of them without their permission. . . .

A More Serious Problem Off-line

Girls are a bit more likely than boys to say that bullying happens more online (33% of girls vs. 25% of boys), though overall, both boys and girls say that kids their age are more likely to be harassed offline. White teens are a bit more likely than African-American teens to think that bullying is more of a problem online—32% of white teens said bullying happens more often online, while 18% of African-American teens said the same. Teens who have online profiles are just as likely as those who do not to say that bullying happens more often offline.

Teens who have been cyberbullied are more likely than their peers who have not been bullied to say that they believe bullying happens online more than offline. However, the majority of bullied teens say that bullying is more likely to happen offline than online. More than 7 in 10 (71%) of teens who have not experienced bullying believe it happens more often offline, while 57% of teens who have been cyberbullied themselves say bullying happens more offline.

> *"The convergence of cheap cellphone and digital cameras, easy-to-use video-sharing Web sites and good old human anarchy has created a whole subgenre: the amateur fight video."*

The Internet Encourages Amateur Fight Videos

Paul Farhi

In the following viewpoint, Paul Farhi, a staff writer for the Washington Post, *describes how Internet video sites are becoming common hosts for violent amateur fight videos. Farhi writes that the Internet allows brawlers a venue for displaying their aggression to a large audience, encouraging others to follow suit in hopes of earning recognition or even money for the sale of fight videos. Farhi notes that the proliferation of these videos is likely to continue because many Web service providers do not restrict them unless users lodge complaints.*

As you read, consider the following questions:

1. According to Farhi, who are "Playas After Cash"?

2. As Farhi reports, why does violence in Internet video postings often "slip past" Web service providers that routinely remove objectionable material from their sites?

3. How does Phil Peplinski defend the posting of fight videos on his Web site, as Farhi relates?

Every now and then, Blake Cater gets an appetite for a fight. There's something about a brawl—a punch-out, a good old-fashioned throwdown—that gets his adrenaline pumping. So with a few of his friends, he goes into his back yard and has at it.

And invites the world to watch.

Armed with a digital video camera, Cater and his friends tape their slugfests and post them on video-sharing Web sites, including Cater's MySpace.com page. The images tell a succinct, brutal story—punches landing squarely on jaws, fists flattening noses, neck-straining headlocks followed by jack-hammer storms of more blows to the face.

Cater says no one has been badly injured—hey, these guys are *friends*—although participants can usually count on some bloody lips, plenty of sore knuckles and a few bruised egos. "I'm not in any way a violent person," says Cater, 22, who lives in Burlington, N.C., "but I enjoy getting out there and fighting when I can."

An Archive of Human Aggression

There's more where that came from. Lots more. The convergence of cheap cellphone and digital cameras, easy-to-use video-sharing Web sites and good old human anarchy has created a whole subgenre: the amateur fight video, now playing all over the Internet. On such sites as YouTube.com or Google Video, you'll increasingly find a treasure-trove—or a cesspool—of people beating on other people, caught on tape by passersby, friends and other photographers. Some of the violence is consensual. Most of it isn't.

Taken together, the fights might be America's unfunniest home videos, an archive of human aggression or a catalogue of stupidity and senselessness. They're also documents of dangerous and illegal behavior, since fighting in public is typically a felony. Although the combatants in fight clips are rarely identified, let alone arrested or punished, fight videos occasionally pop up on the police blotter.

In Arlington, Tex. [in May 2006], police arrested six men and boys, allegedly members of a gang called Playas After Cash, for arranging street fights and selling DVDs of the mayhem over the Internet; a 16-year-old participant in one of the recorded fights was hospitalized with a brain hemorrhage. And in April [2006], a seven-minute video of two girls fighting in Fresno—while one of the girls' mothers watched—led to a flurry of news reports and a police investigation of the mother for child endangerment (the girls were suspended from school).

There are grainy videos of men belting, head-butting and kicking other men, and shaky camera shots of girls and women hitting, scratching and stomping each other. The soundtrack is usually the excited voices of spectators, but many of the clips have been set to music (usually hip hop or thrash metal). Most are devoid of context or explanation, or even provocation.

The settings are anyplace and everywhere. One arm-flailing fight takes place between surfers offshore. And a three-minute video of a Russian street brawl appears to pit two small armies of young men. As the camera rolls, the two mobs move toward each other at a slow walk, then combust into anarchy.

Web Service Providers Rely on User Complaints

In interviews, representatives of video-sharing Web sites seemed only vaguely aware that fight videos are being posted on their services. A few even needed the concept explained to them.

All the major Web services employ teams of people to scour user postings and remove objectionable material. But since nudity and sexually oriented videos command the most attention, violence often slips past.

Google Video has no specific prohibition on clips featuring fighting, but Peter Chane, business products manager for the site, says his company will flag videos "in which someone is hurt or someone dies." Except that the extent of injuries in fight videos isn't always clear. Google Video, in any event, hosts plenty of mayhem, including brawls that leave participants motionless and apparently unconscious. "We try to be as open as possible," Chane says. "Our number one goal is to get as much content online as possible, as long as it doesn't offend."

YouTube, the most popular file-sharing site (it receives about 40,000 homemade videos a day), says it leaves the flagging to its users. The site bans those who've been repeatedly cited for inappropriate postings. But its rules about violent videos are vague. Those submitting their work to the site agree, according to its Terms of Use statement, not to submit "material that is unlawful, obscene, defamatory, libelous, threatening, pornographic, harassing, hateful, racially or ethnically offensive, or encourages conduct that would be considered a criminal offense, give rise to civil liability, violate any law, or is otherwise inappropriate."

"It's all subject to what the community [of YouTube users] feels is appropriate," says Julie Supan, senior director of marketing. She adds: "We've removed a lot of fights [because of user complaints]. This service has a very broad demographic of users, and we're focused on making it an enjoyable place for everyone."

Watching Violence on the Net

A quick scan of YouTube suggests it can be a pretty rough place. Here's a video of a preadolescent girl smacking another

Violent Videos Earn Prices Online

At Break.com, site owner Keith Richman holds video popularity contests and pays the winners. Last year, he paid $500 for rights to video of a dry ice bomb blowing up in a man's hand, according to Charlie Dyess—the man featured in the video.

The four-minute-long movie shows a group of men and teenagers in a warehouse in Alexandria, La., making "dry ice bombs." When one failed to explode despite repeated attempts to trigger a blast, the 38-year-old Dyess picked it up. It exploded immediately.

"At first, I thought my fingers were gone. I thought I blew them off," Dyess said. Shrapnel from the bottle tore into his arm, and he temporarily lost hearing in his right ear.

Dyess recovered, and not long after, he and the man behind the camera—friend Jason Rogers—decided to enter Break.com's contest. They won second place, good for $500, he said.

Bob Sullivan, *"Gruesome Stunts, Risky Pranks Mar Video Sites,"*
MSNBC, June 21, 2006. http://redtape.msnbc.com.

girl repeatedly in the face. Here's the infamous and unexplained Moscow gang brawl, complete with bodies falling to the ground amid the exploding violence. Here's an ugly schoolyard fight, labeled "Mississippi Brawl."

The Mississippi video is one of about 500 fight videos collected by Phil Peplinski, 46, a martial-arts instructor in central Florida. Peplinski maintains a Web site (Comegetyou some.com) that contains a portion of his collection and acts as a kind of magnet for fight fanatics and fight tapers.

Peplinski says the point of the site isn't lurid entertainment, but rather instruction. "Most people have never been in a [physical] confrontation," he says. "They have difficulty understanding true violence. I'm hoping people will learn what to do when faced with the real thing."

What they should do, he says, is "walk away."

Decades of social-science research have confirmed that prolonged exposure to violence on TV can lead to a loss of sensitivity about violent acts, a heightened fear of strangers and sometimes aggressive or copycat behavior. But the effects of watching it online are less understood because Internet violence hasn't been studied as closely, says Kathryn Montgomery, a communications professor at American University in Northwest Washington who has written extensively about television and children.

"Kids have a different relationship [to the Internet] than to a TV set," she points out. "It's not as passive. You're not just sitting in a room being mesmerized by images. You can interact with the content [online], you can reply to it and you can create it. But we just don't know if it affects them the same way television does. It's a murky area."

Peplinski doesn't believe taping violence for others to watch begets more violence, or even more taping. "It's all self-perpetuation," he says. "Look at all the cameras that come out when a fight starts. This is the unfortunate and sad part. Humans have a propensity toward violence. Period. The only thing that has changed is the ability to record it."

Peplinski doesn't sell his fight footage, but others do. The Internet is rife with marketers of street-brawl DVD collections, with such titles as "Bare Knuckle Beatdowns," "Extreme Chick Fights" and "Felony Fights."

Marketing Violent Videos

A site called Realfight.com, which sells a series of DVDs called "Ghetto Fights," entreats would-be customers with this statement: "Are these fights 'real'? Yes, our team has literally searched the globe for only the best footage. None of the fights are staged like you might find in wrestling or fighting championship tapes. In fact, none of these fights have every [sic] been seen anywhere else." The company did not respond to several calls left on its answering machine.

Fights and fight tapes are practically a given among some European soccer fans, says Rogier Both, a fan and frequent fighter who lives in the Dutch city of Haarlem. Indeed, DVD collections of British soccer hooligan fights are copious. "There are always people looking to fight" before big games, he says. "There is always, every day, someone to fight with."

Both, 21, is more than happy to oblige. He'll often meet other young supporters of his home team at the local train station on game days. As they walk together to the stadium, they'll brawl with rival fans they meet along the way and tape the results. His frequent duke-outs earned him a two-year ban from games throughout the Netherlands, he reports (the ban ended this season). Still, Both, who is an account manager for an online company, is quick to add: "I am not a hooligan. I may go to fight, but I go for the football, too."

Like Blake Cater, Both says he likes fighting for the "adrenaline kick," and also for the camaraderie and community with his fellow fans and fighters. The tapes of their melees are like old game films, to be shared and savored: "We look through them, like at a birthday or when we are having a beer," he says.

"It's like an addiction," he adds. "You can't leave it. When there is a good football fight, the best sex is not better. . . . People who have never been in football matches in Europe will never understand it, but it's like a second life."

Both might want to ring up Cater. Since moving to North Carolina from West Virginia this year, Cater has been trying to recruit new friends for some more backyard brawling. "I would absolutely do it again," he says. "It was always fun for all of us."

Plus, he adds, "everyone I've shown the footage to has enjoyed it as well."

> "A 10 percent increase in Net access yields about a 7.3 percent decrease in reported rapes."

The Internet Reduces Violent Criminal Behavior

Steven E. Landsburg

Steven E. Landsburg is a professor of economics at the University of Rochester in New York. He is also a regular columnist for Forbes *and* Slate *magazines, as well as the author of* More Sex Is Safer Sex: The Unconventional Wisdom of Economics. *In the following viewpoint, Landsburg explains the results of university experiments that measured the impact of onscreen sex and violence on violent crime rates. According to these studies, increasing access to pornography on the Internet reduced reports of rape, and the release of violent movies in theaters correlated with a decrease in violent crimes. Landsburg states that these findings question the commonly held belief that violent images tend to incite people to act out violence in the real world.*

As you read, consider the following questions:

1. Why does Professor Todd Kendall conclude that it is most likely access to pornography on the Internet that deters rapists from committing crimes?

2. Why does Landsburg argue that the "most probable explanation" for the drop in violent crime rates is due to the fact that violent criminals prefer watching violent movies to committing crimes?

3. In Landsburg's view, what is the "right question" to ask when trying to assess the impact of on-screen violence on real-world violence?

Does pornography breed rape? Do violent movies breed violent crime? Quite the opposite, it seems.

First, porn. What happens when more people view more of it? The rise of the Internet offers a gigantic natural experiment. Better yet, because Internet usage caught on at different times in different states, it offers 50 natural experiments.

The bottom line on these experiments is, "More Net access, less rape." A 10 percent increase in Net access yields about a 7.3 percent decrease in reported rapes. States that adopted the Internet quickly saw the biggest declines. And, according to Clemson professor Todd Kendall, the effects remain even after you control for all of the obvious confounding variables, such as alcohol consumption, police presence, poverty and unemployment rates, population density, and so forth.

A Substitute Effect

OK, so we can at least tentatively conclude that Net access reduces rape. But that's a far cry from proving that *porn* access reduces rape. Maybe rape is down because the rapists are all indoors reading *Slate* or vandalizing Wikipedia. But professor Kendall points out that there is no similar effect of Internet access on homicide. It's hard to see how Wikipedia can deter rape without deterring other violent crimes at the same time. On the other hand, it's easy to imagine how porn might serve as a substitute for rape.

If not Wikipedia, then what? Maybe rape is down because former rapists have found their true loves on Match.com. But

Changes in Rape and Homicide Incidence as a Function of Internet Growth, 1998–2003

	Rapes per 100,000 Residents			
	1990	1995	2003	2003–1995
26 Quick Adopting States	35.6	33.6	28.9	−4.7 (−14%)
25 Slow Adopting States	44.0	42.3	39.8	−2.5 (−5.9%)
Difference	−8.4	−8.7	−10.9	−2.2

	Homicides per 100,000 Residents			
	1990	1995	2003	2003–1995
26 Quick Adopting States	6.31	5.89	4.16	−1.73 (−29.4%)
25 Slow Adopting States	10.62	9.96	6.92	−3.04 (−30.4%)
Difference	−4.31	−4.07	−2.76	+1.31

Note: States are classified into the 26 states with the fastest growth in internet usage, and the other 25 states. The difference in rape and homicide between the two groups is similar in 1990 and 1995, before home access to the internet became widespread. However, by 2003, the Quick Adopting states' rape incidence rate fell significantly more than the Slow Adopting states' rate. Such a pattern is not, however, evident for homicide.

TAKEN FROM: Todd Kendall, "Pornography, Rape, and the Internet," September 28, 2006.

professor Kendall points out that the effects are strongest among 15-year-old to 19-year-old perpetrators—the group least likely to use such dating services.

Moreover, professor Kendall argues that those teenagers are precisely the group that (presumably) relies most heavily on the Internet for access to porn. When you're living with your parents, it's a lot easier to close your browser in a hurry than to hide a stash of magazines. So, the auxiliary evidence is all consistent with the hypothesis that Net access reduces rape because Net access makes it easy to find porn.

Violent Videos Reduce Violent Crime

Next, violence. What happens when a particularly violent movie is released? Answer: Violent crime rates fall. Instantly.

Here again, we have a lot of natural experiments: The number of violent movie releases changes a lot from week to week. One weekend, 12 million people watch *Hannibal,* and another weekend, 12 million watch *Wallace & Gromit: The Curse of the Were-Rabbit.*

University of California professors Gordon Dahl and Stefano Della Vigna compared what happens on those weekends. The bottom line: More violence on the screen means less violence in the streets. Probably that's because violent criminals prefer violent movies, and as long as they're at the movies, they're not out causing mischief. They'd rather see *Hannibal* than rob you, but they'd rather rob you than sit through *Wallace & Gromit.*

I say that's the most probable explanation, because the biggest drop in crime (about a 2 percent drop for every million people watching violent movies) occurs between 6 P.M. and midnight—the prime moviegoing hours. And what happens when the theaters close? Answer: Crime stays down, though not by quite as much. Dahl and Della Vigna speculate that this is because two hours at the movies means two hours of drinking Coke instead of beer, with sobering effects that persist right on through till morning. Speaking of morning, after 6 A.M., crime returns to its original level.

What about those experiments you learned about in freshman psych, where subjects exposed to violent images were more willing to turn up the voltage on actors who they believed were receiving painful electric shocks? Those experiments demonstrate, perhaps, that most people become more violent after viewing violent images. But that's the wrong question here. The right question is: Do *the sort of people who commit violent crimes* commit more crimes when they watch violence? And the answer appears to be no, for the simple reason that they can't commit crimes and watch movies simultaneously.

Look at the Data

Similarly, psychologists have found that male subjects, immediately after watching pornography, are more likely to express misogynistic attitudes. But as professor Kendall points out, we need to be clear on what those experiments are testing: They are testing the effects of watching pornography in a controlled laboratory setting under the eyes of a researcher. The experience of viewing porn on the Internet, in the privacy of one's own room, typically culminates in a slightly messier but far more satisfying experience—an experience that could plausibly tamp down some of the same aggressions that the *pornus interruptus* of the laboratory tends to stir up.

In other words, if you want to understand the effects of on-screen sex and violence outside the laboratory, psych experiments don't tell you very much. Sooner or later, you've got to look at the data.

> *"By its very nature, the Internet is in many ways an ideal arena for activity by terrorist organizations."*

Terrorists Are Using the Internet to Further Their Violent Aims

Gabriel Weimann

In the following viewpoint, Gabriel Weimann explains how terrorist groups utilize the Internet to further their aims. Weimann states that ease of access, anonymity, and lack of regulation make the Internet an ideal venue for terrorists to recruit, fundraise, and collect information on potential targets. Weimann also maintains that terrorists use the Internet as a weapon to launch propaganda and fear campaigns. Finally, he points out that the networking capabilities of the Internet allow disparate terrorist cells to keep in touch and coordinate attacks. Gabriel Weimann is professor of communication at Haifa University in Israel. He is also a senior fellow at the United States Institute of Peace, a congressionally funded research institute that promotes peaceful resolutions to violent conflicts around the globe.

Gabriel Weimann, *www.terror.net: How Modern Terrorism Uses the Internet.* Washington, DC: United States Institute of Peace, 2004. www.usip.org. Reproduced by permission.

As you read, consider the following questions:

1. What are the three basic audiences for terrorist Web sites, according to Weimann?
2. What is "cyberfear," as Weimann explains it?
3. As Weimann relates, how do terrorists use the Internet to recruit members?

The story of the presence of terrorists groups in cyberspace has barely begun to be told. In 1998, around half of the thirty organizations designated as "Foreign Terrorist Organizations" under the U.S. Antiterrorism and Effective Death Penalty Act of 1996 maintained Web sites; by 2000, virtually all terrorist groups had established their presence on the Internet. Our scan of the Internet in 2003–4 revealed hundreds of Web sites serving terrorists and their supporters. And yet, despite this growing terrorist presence, when policy makers, journalists, and academics have discussed the combination of terrorism and the Internet, they have focused on the overrated threat posed by cyberterrorism or cyberwarfare (i.e., attacks on computer networks, including those on the Internet) and largely ignored the numerous uses that terrorists make of the Internet every day. . . .

By its very nature, the Internet is in many ways an ideal arena for activity by terrorist organizations. Most notably, it offers

- easy access;
- little or no regulation, censorship, or other forms of government control;
- potentially huge audiences spread throughout the world;
- anonymity of communication;
- fast flow of information;

- inexpensive development and maintenance of a Web presence;

- a multimedia environment (the ability to combine text, graphics, audio, and video and to allow users to download films, songs, books, posters, and so forth); and

- the ability to shape coverage in the traditional mass media, which increasingly use the Internet as a source for stories. . . .

The Audience for Terrorist Web Sites

What is the content of terrorist sites? Typically, a site will provide a history of the organization and its activities, a detailed review of its social and political background, accounts of its notable exploits, biographies of its leaders, founders, and heroes, information on its political and ideological aims, fierce criticism of its enemies, and up-to-date news. Nationalist and separatist organizations generally display maps of the areas in dispute: the Hamas [Islamic Resistance Movement] site shows a map of Palestine, the FARC [Armed Revolutionary Forces of Colombia] site shows a map of Colombia, the LTTE [Liberation Tigers of Tamil Ealam] site presents a map of Sri Lanka, and so forth. Despite the ever-present vocabulary of "the armed struggle" and "resistance," what most sides do *not* feature is a detailed description of their violent activities. Even if they expound at length on the moral and legal basis of the legitimacy of the use of violence, most sites refrain from referring to the terrorists' violent actions or their fatal consequences—this reticence is presumably inspired by propagandist and image-building considerations. Two exceptions to this rule are Hezbollah and Hamas, whose sites feature updated statistical reports of their actions ("daily operations") and tallies of both "dead martyrs" and "Israeli enemies" and "collaborators" killed.

Whom do the Internet terrorists target at their sites? An analysis of the content of the Web sites suggests three different audiences.

- *Current and potential supporters.* Terrorist Web sites make heavy use of slogans and offer items for sale, including T-shirts, badges, flags, and videotapes and audiocassettes, all evidently aimed at sympathizers. Often, an organization will target its local supporters with a site in the local language and will provide detailed information about the activities and internal politics of the organization, its allies, and its competitors.

- *International public opinion.* The international public, who are not directly involved in the conflict but who may have some interest in the issues involved, are courted with sites in languages other than the local tongue. Most sites offer versions in several languages. ETA's [Basque separatist movement] site, for instance, offers information in Castilian, German, French, and Italian; the MRTA [Peruvian Tupak-Amaru Revolutionary Movement] site offers Japanese and Italian in addition to its English and Spanish versions; and the IMU [Islamic Movement of Uzbekistan] site uses Arabic, English, and Russian. For the benefit of their international audiences, the sites present basic information about the organization and extensive historical background material (material with which the organization's supporters are presumably already familiar).

Judging from the content of many of the sites, it appears that foreign journalists are also targeted. Press releases are often placed on the Web sites in an effort to get the organization's point of view into the traditional media. The detailed background information is also very useful for international reporters. One of Hezbollah's sites specifically addresses journalists, inviting them to interact with the organization's press office via e-mail.

- *Enemy publics.* Efforts to reach enemy publics (i.e., citizens of the states against which the terrorists are fighting) are not as clearly apparent from the content of many sites. However, some sites do seem to make an effort to demoralize the enemy by threatening attacks and by fostering feelings of guilt about the enemy's conduct and motives. In the process, they also seek to stimulate public debate in their enemies' states, to change public opinion, and to weaken public support for the governing regime.

How Terrorists Use the Internet

We have identified eight different, albeit sometimes overlapping, ways in which contemporary terrorists use the Internet. Some of these parallel the uses to which everyone puts the Internet—information gathering, for instance. Some resemble the uses made of the medium by traditional political organizations—for example, raising funds and disseminating propaganda. Others, however, are much more unusual and distinctive—for instance, hiding instructions, manuals, and directions in coded messages or encrypted files.

Psychological Warfare. Terrorism has often been conceptualized as a form of psychological warfare, and certainly terrorists have sought to wage such a campaign through the Internet. There are several ways for terrorists to do so. For instance, they can use the Internet to spread disinformation, to deliver threats intended to distill fear and helplessness, and to disseminate horrific images of recent actions, such as the brutal murder of the American journalist Daniel Pearl [in 2002] by his captors [a group calling itself the National Movement for the Restoration of Pakistani Sovereignty], a videotape of which was replayed on several terrorist Web sites. Terrorists can also launch psychological attacks through cyberterrorism, or, more accurately, through creating the fear of cyberterrorism. "Cyberfear" is generated when concern about what a computer attack *could* do (for example, bringing down airliners by disabling air traffic control systems, or disrupting national economies by wrecking the computerized systems that regulate stock markets) is amplified until the public believes that an attack *will* happen. The Internet—an uncensored medium that carries stories, pictures, threats, or messages regardless of their validity or potential impact—is peculiarly well suited to allowing even a small group to amplify its message and exaggerate its importance and the threat it poses.

Al Qaeda combines multimedia propaganda and advanced communication technologies to create a very sophisticated form of psychological warfare. Osama bin Laden and his followers concentrate their propaganda efforts on the Internet, where visitors to al Qaeda's numerous Web sites and to the sites of sympathetic, aboveground organizations can access prerecorded videotapes and audiotapes, CD-ROMs, DVDs, photographs, and announcements. Despite the massive onslaught it has sustained in recent years—the arrests and deaths of many of its members, the dismantling of its operational bases and training camps in Afghanistan, and the smashing of its bases in the Far East—al Qaeda has been able to conduct an impressive scare campaign. Since September 11, 2001, the organization has festooned its Web sites with a string of announcements of an impending "large attack" on U.S. targets. These warnings have received considerable media coverage, which has helped to generate a widespread sense of dread and insecurity among audiences throughout the world and especially within the United States. . . .

Publicity and Propaganda. The Internet has significantly expanded the opportunities for terrorists to secure publicity. Until the advent of the Internet, terrorists' hopes of winning publicity for their causes and activities depended on attracting the attention of television, radio, or the print media. These traditional media have "selection thresholds" (multistage processes of editorial selection) that terrorists often cannot reach. No such thresholds, of course, exist on the terrorists' own Web sites. The fact that many terrorists now have direct control over the content of their message offers further opportunities to shape how they are perceived by different target audiences and to manipulate their own image and the image of their enemies.

As noted earlier, most terrorist sites do not celebrate their violent activities. Instead, regardless of the terrorists' agendas, motives, and location, most sites emphasize two issues: the restrictions placed on freedom of expression and the plight of comrades who are now political prisoners. These issues resonate powerfully with their own supporters and are also calculated to elicit sympathy from Western audiences that cherish freedom of expression and frown on measures to silence political opposition. Enemy publics, too, may be targets for these complaints insofar as the terrorists, by emphasizing the antidemocratic nature of the steps taken against them, try to create feelings of unease and shame among their foes. The terrorists' protest at being muzzled, it may be noted, is particularly well suited to the Internet, which for many users is *the* symbol of free, unfettered, and uncensored communication. . . .

Data Mining. The Internet may be viewed as a vast digital library. The World Wide Web alone offers about a billion pages of information, much of it free—and much of it of interest to terrorist organizations. Terrorists, for instance, can learn from the Internet a wide variety of details about targets such as transportation facilities, nuclear power plants, public buildings, airports, and ports, and even about counterterrorism measures. Dan Verton, in his book *Black Ice: The Invisible Threat of Cyberterrorism* (2003), explains that "al Qaeda cells now operate with the assistance of large databases containing details of potential targets in the U.S. They use the Internet to collect intelligence on those targets, especially critical economic nodes, and modern software enables them to study structural weaknesses in facilities as well as predict the cascading failure effect of attacking certain systems." According to Secretary of Defense Donald Rumsfeld, speaking on January 15, 2003, an al Qaeda training manual recovered in Afghanistan tells its readers, "Using public sources openly and without resorting to illegal means, it is possible to gather at least 80 percent of all information required about the enemy."

The Web site operated by the Muslim Hackers Club (a group that U.S. security agencies believe aims to develop software tools with which to launch cyberattacks) has featured links to U.S. sites that purport to disclose sensitive information such as code names and radio frequencies used by the U.S. Secret Service. The same Web site offers tutorials in creating and spreading viruses, devising hacking stratagems, sabotaging networks, and developing codes; it also provides links to other militant Islamic and terrorist Web addresses. Specific targets that al Qaeda-related Web sites have discussed include the Centers for Disease Control and Prevention in Atlanta; FedWire, the money-movement clearing system maintained by the Federal Reserve Board; and facilities controlling the flow of information over the Internet. Like many other Internet users, terrorists have access not only to maps and diagrams of potential targets but also to imaging data on those same facilities and networks that may reveal counterterrorist activities at a target site. One captured al Qaeda computer contained engineering and structural features of a dam, which had been downloaded from the Internet and which would enable al Qaeda engineers and planners to simulate catastrophic failures. In other captured computers, U.S. investigators found evidence that al Qaeda operators spent time on sites that offer software and programming instructions for the digital switches that run power, water, transportation, and communications grids. . . .

Fundraising. Like many other political organizations, terrorist groups use the Internet to raise funds. Al Qaeda, for instance, has always depended heavily on donations, and its global fund-raising network is built upon a foundation of charities, nongovernmental organizations, and other financial institutions that use Web sites and Internet-based chat rooms and forums. The Sunni extremist group Hizb al-Tahrir uses an integrated web of Internet sites, stretching from Europe to Africa, which asks supporters to assist the effort by giving money and encouraging others to donate to the cause of jihad. Banking information, including the numbers of accounts into which donations can be deposited, is provided on a site based in Germany. The fighters in the Russian breakaway republic of Chechnya have likewise used the Internet to publicize the numbers of bank accounts to which sympathizers can contribute. (One of these Chechen bank accounts is located in Sacramento, California.) The IRA's [Irish Republican Army] Web site contains a page on which visitors can make credit card donations. . . .

Recruitment and Mobilization. The Internet can be used not only to solicit donations from sympathizers but also to recruit and mobilize supporters to play a more active role in support of terrorist activities or causes. In addition to seeking converts by using the full panoply of Web site technologies (audio, digital video, etc.) to enhance the presentation of their message, terrorist organizations capture information about the users who browse their Web sites. Users who seem most interested in the organization's cause or well suited to carrying out its work are then contacted. Recruiters may also use more interactive Internet technology to roam online chat rooms and cybercafes, looking for receptive members of the public, par-

The Threat of al Qaeda Cyber-Attacks

Terrorists are targeting our cyber infrastructure and we have got to educate the public about this threat. According to news reports, data from al Qaeda computers found in Afghanistan show that the group had scouted systems that control critical U.S. infrastructure. An attack on these systems could have devastating results, especially if done in conjunction with a physical attack.

A study by the National Infrastructure Protection Center concluded that the effects of September 11 [2001] would have been far greater if launched in conjunction with a cyber attack disabling New York City's water or electrical systems. An attack on these systems would have inhibited emergency services from dealing with the crisis and turned many of the spectators into victims.

Jon Kyl, opening statement at a hearing before the Senate Subcommittee on Terrorism, Technology and Homeland Security, February 24, 2004.

ticularly young people. Electronic bulletin boards and user nets (issue-specific chat rooms and bulletins) can also serve as vehicles for reaching out to potential recruits. . . .

Networking. Many terrorist groups, among them Hamas and al Qaeda, have undergone a transformation from strictly hierarchical organizations with designated leaders to affiliations of semi-independent cells that have no single commanding hierarchy. Through the use of the Internet, these loosely interconnected groups are able to maintain contact with one another— and with members of other terrorist groups. In the future, terrorists are increasingly to be organized in a more decentralized manner, with arrays of transnational groups linked by the Internet and communicating and coordinating horizontally rather than vertically. . . .

Sharing Information. The World Wide Web is home to dozens of sites that provide information on how to build chemical and explosive weapons. Many of these sites post *The Terrorist's Handbook* and *The Anarchist Cookbook*, two well-known manuals that offer detailed instructions on how to construct a wide range of bombs. Another manual, *The Mujahadeen Poisons Handbook*, written by Abdel-Aziz in 1996 and "published" on the official Hamas Web site, details in twenty-three pages how to prepare various homemade poisons, poisonous gases, and other deadly materials for use in terrorist attacks. A much larger manual, nicknamed "The Encyclopedia of Jihad" and prepared by al Qaeda, runs to thousands of pages; distributed through the Internet, it offers detailed instructions on how to establish an underground organization and execute attacks. One al Qaeda laptop found in Afghanistan had been used to make multiple visits to a French site run by the Société Anonyme (a self-described "fluctuating group of artists and theoreticians who work specifically on the relations between critical thinking and artistic practices"), which offers a two-volume *Sabotage Handbook* with sections on topics such as planning an assassination and antisurveillance methods. . . .

Planning and Coordination. Terrorists use the Internet not only to learn how to build bombs but also to plan and coordinate specific attacks. Al Qaeda operatives relied heavily on the Internet in planning and coordinating the September 11 attacks. Thousands of encrypted messages that had been posted in a password-protected area of a Web site were found by federal officials on the computer of arrested al Qaeda terrorist Abu Zubaydah, who reportedly masterminded the September 11 attacks. The first messages found on Zubaydah's computer were dated May 2001 and the last were sent on September 9, 2001. The frequency of the messages was highest in August 2001. To preserve their anonymity, the al Qaeda terrorists used the Internet in public places and sent messages via public e-mail. Some of the September 11 hijackers communicated using free Web-based e-mail accounts.

Hamas activists in the Middle East, for example, use chat rooms to plan operations and operatives exchange e-mail to coordinate actions across Gaza, the West Bank, Lebanon, and Israel. Instructions in the form of maps, photographs, directions, and technical details of how to use explosives are often disguised by means of steganography, which involves hiding messages inside graphic files. Sometimes, however, instructions are delivered concealed in only the simplest of codes. Mohammed Atta's final message to the other eighteen terrorists who carried out the attacks of 9/11 is reported to have read: "The semester begins in three more weeks. We've obtained 19 confirmations for studies in the faculty of law, the faculty of urban planning, the faculty of fine arts, and the faculty of engineering." (The reference to the various faculties was apparently the code for the buildings targeted in the attacks.) . . .

Using the Advantages of the Internet to Achieve Terrorist Goals

In a briefing given in late September 2001, Ronald Dick, assistant director of the FBI and head of the United States National Infrastructure Protection Center (NIPC), told reporters that the hijackers of 9/11 had used the Internet, and "used it well." Since 9/11, terrorists have only sharpened their Internet skills and increased their Web presence. Today, terrorists of very different ideological persuasions—Islamist, Marxist, nationalist, separatist, racist—have learned many of the same lessons about how to make the most of the Internet. The great virtues of the Internet—ease of access, lack of regulation, vast potential audiences, fast flow of information, and so forth— have been turned to the advantage of groups committed to terrorizing societies to achieve their goals.

Periodical Bibliography

The following articles have been selected to supplement the diverse views presented in this chapter.

Atlantic Monthly	"Waving the Bloody JPEG," October 2004.
Christopher Dickey	"Inside the Cyber-Jihad," *Newsweek*, July 30, 2007.
Thomas L. Friedman	"Barney and Baghdad," *New York Times*, October 18, 2006.
Sameer Hinduja and Justin W. Patchin	"Offline Consequences of Online Victimization: School Violence and Delinquency," *Journal of School Violence*, 6.3, 2007.
Phil McKenna	"The Rise of Cyberbullying," *New Scientist*, July 21, 2007.
Jonathan Milne	"What Have We Got To Be Scared Of?" *Times Educational Supplement*, January 25, 2008.
New York Times	"Teenagers Misbehaving, for All Online to Watch," February 13, 2007.
Jamie Reno	"Over the (Border) Line," *Newsweek*, May 8, 2006.
Nicole Rosenleaf Ritter	"Cyber-Bullies R 4 Real," *Woman's Day*, February 1, 2007.
Sue Tait	"Pornographies of Violence? Internet Spectatorship on Body Horror," *Critical Studies in Media Communication*, March 2008.
Henry Walpole	"Video Bullies Can Do Your Head In," *Times Educational Supplement*, August 17, 2007.

For Further Discussion

Chapter 1

1. In his viewpoint, Henry Jenkins contends that violent media may have an effect on individuals, yet he makes the claim that "there is no such thing as media violence." What does Jenkins mean by his bold assertion? Do you think his argument is reasonable? Explain how Jenkins's opinion has or has not changed your view of the effects of media violence on individuals and society.

2. After reading the viewpoints by David S. Bickham and Christopher J. Ferguson, explain whether you believe violence in video games leads to aggressive behavior in the players. Point out the arguments in the viewpoints that you think were most convincing in shaping your opinion.

3. James Bowman asserts that much of the violence perpetrated by heroes in modern movies lacks a moral dimension. Thus, violence becomes its own aesthetic, divorced from any notion of right and wrong. Do you think Bowman's argument is persuasive? Referencing films you've seen in the last few years, explain whether you agree or disagree with Bowman's claim.

Chapter 2

1. The government currently bans the broadcasting of indecent material on public airwaves because it is of "slight social value" and because it supposedly has a harmful effect on the well-being of children. In this manner, the government has circumscribed the First Amendment by placing public welfare before free expression. The Federal Communications Commission asserts that based on the same principal argument, lawmakers could restrict exces-

sively violent material on public airwaves. Do you think this argument is valid? Explain your answer.

2. Rejecting calls for government intervention, both Adam Thierer and Kerry Howley contend that parents should maintain the power to restrict the types of television programming that reach children. The two authors acknowledge that parents already have the tools to judge and block programming, but they seem to have differing views on the value of these tools. Using quotes from Thierer's and Howley's viewpoints, explain the ways in which their arguments are similar and different.

3. After reading the viewpoints by Patricia E. Vance and Jonathan Harbour, explain whether you believe the ESRB ratings system is an asset to parents trying to determine what video games are appropriate for their children. Defend your opinion, in part, by showing how the opposing viewpoint fails to convince. You may also use personal experience with the ESRB system to support your argument.

Chapter 3

1. Kristin Goldberg Goff argues that television news stories about violence are particularly scary for children. Do you think her assertion is correct—namely, that the repetition of such news events may lead children to believe the world is a violent and frightening place? In your own experience, has the abundance of violent news made you feel that the world—or even your own community—is hostile and scary? Explain your answer. You may reference other articles in the chapter to support your opinions.

2. Clive Thompson makes the claim that government policy is sometimes guided by television—especially the rhetoric of tough, heroic dramas and thrillers. Do you agree with

his assessment? Provide examples of when government policy has seemed to mirror fictional narratives of popular television programs or films.

Chapter 4

1. Drawing from personal experience or from secondhand stories from friends, explain whether you think cyber-bullying is a more destructive form of intimidation than traditional bullying is. Cull support from the viewpoints by Amanda Lenhart and Scott Meech and explain which of their conclusions seem accurate based on your own understanding of the problem.

2. After reading the viewpoint by Paul Farhi, explain whether you believe major Web service providers should do more to expel videotaped fights and brawls from their viewer libraries? If so, how should this be accomplished? (Make sure you address the ways sites use to filter content, as Farhi notes.) If you do not advocate the removal of fight videos, how do you support their inclusion in these major posting sites?

3. Steven E. Landsburg's viewpoint reiterates the findings of Todd Kendall, the Clemson professor who concludes that the availability of pornography and violence in movies and on the Internet can deter the criminally minded from committing acts of rape or violence in the real world. After clearly explaining how Kendall makes his argument, tell whether you agree or disagree with his conclusion. If you agree with his view, do you think this is a reason to oppose restrictions on media violence?

Organizations to Contact

The editors have compiled the following list of organizations concerned with the issues debated in this book. The descriptions are derived from materials provided by the organizations. All have publications or information available for interested readers. The list was compiled on the date of publication of the present volume; the information provided here may change. Be aware that many organizations take several weeks or longer to respond to inquiries, so allow as much time as possible.

American Civil Liberties Union (ACLU)
125 Broad St., 18th Floor, New York, NY 10004
(212) 549-2500
E-mail: aclu@aclu.org
Web site: www.aclu.org

The American Civil Liberties Union (ACLU) works to ensure that there are no infringements upon the rights guaranteed to all U.S. citizens by the Declaration of Independence and the Constitution. Accordingly, the organization is opposed to the censoring of any form of speech, including depictions of violence in the media. Handbooks, project and public policy reports, pamphlets, and other publications by the ACLU are all available on the organization's Web site.

American Psychological Association (APA)
750 First St. NE, Washington, DC 20002
(800) 374-2721
E-mail: public.affairs@apa.org
Web site: www.apa.org

The American Psychological Association (APA), a professional society of psychologists, seeks to promote the field of psychology as a science and profession and to encourage its utilization to better human life and society as a whole. The association has conducted numerous studies causally linking exposure to media violence and violent behavior and aggression. The APA advocates strongly for a reduction of violent content in video games and other media and supports content-based ratings warning consumers of the level of portrayed violence. Numerous reports, press releases, and journal articles concerning all aspects of the impact of media violence are available on the APA's Web site.

Canadians Concerned About Violence in Entertainment (C-CAVE)

167 Glen Rd., Toronto, ON   M4W 2W8
  Canada
E-mail: info@c-cave.com
Web site: www.c-cave.com

Canadians Concerned About Violence in Entertainment (C-CAVE) aims to educate the public about the impact of media violence on society. The organization provides general information to the public through its Web site as well as by participating in public forums and lectures. C-CAVE views increased media literacy, in combination with sensible government regulations and self-regulation of the entertainment industry, as the cornerstones of achieving a safer society. The C-CAVE Web site offers numerous articles and links to other organizations combating violent entertainment.

Cato Institute

1000 Massachusetts Ave. NW, Washington, DC   20001
(202) 842-0200 • Fax: (202) 842-3490
E-mail: cato@cato.org
Web site: www.cato.org

As a libertarian, public policy research institution, the Cato Institute is committed to promoting limited government, individual liberties, and a free-market economy. As such, it also opposes the regulation of television and other media violence by the government. Publications of the organization include the quarterly *Regulation* magazine, the bimonthly *Cato Policy Report*, and the periodic *Cato Journal*.

Center for Media Literacy (CML)
23852 Pacific Coast Hwy., #472, Malibu, CA   90265
(310) 456-1225 • Fax: (310) 456-0020
E-mail: cml@medialit.org
Web site: www.medialit.org

The Center for Media Literacy (CML) promotes media literacy, a critical analysis of the media and media content, as the most effective means of combating the negative effects of media violence. CML believes that if individuals begin to look critically at the media from a young age, they will learn to make good choices about what media they choose to engage with and mediate any negative impact. *C*O*N*N*E*C*T* is the periodic newsletter of the organization, and archives of the magazine *Media & Values* (1977–1993) are available on the CML's Web site.

Entertainment Software Ratings Board (ESRB)
317 Madison Ave., 22nd Floor, New York, NY   10017
Web site: www.esrb.org

The Entertainment Software Ratings Board (ESRB) serves as the self-regulatory body of the entertainment software industry, providing standardized ratings for all video and computer games. These ratings provide consumers with information about the content of the games and suggest the age range for which the games are most appropriate. Ratings guides and public service announcements have all been created to help the public become more informed about the value and meaning of the ratings.

Federal Communications Commission (FCC)
445 Twelfth St. SW, Washington, DC   20554
(888) 225-5322 • Fax: (866) 418-0232
E-mail: fccinfo@fcc.gov
Web site: www.fcc.gov

The Federal Communications Commission (FCC), an independent government agency, regulates telecommunications within the United States. It is responsible for creating and implementing policies for interstate and international communication by radio, television, wire, satellite, and cable. Additionally, the FCC reviews all educational programming created by the networks. Reports, updates, and reviews published by the FCC are accessible on the commission's Web site.

The First Amendment Center
1207 Eighteenth Ave. S, Nashville, TN   37212
(615) 727-1600 • Fax: (615) 727-1319
E-mail: info@fac.org
Web site: www.firstamendmentcenter.org

The First Amendment Center champions the rights of all Americans and the media, as guaranteed by the First Amendment of the Constitution. The organization provides information to the public and members of the government to ensure that First Amendment rights are always observed. The center's Web site offers up-to-date information about current legislation and policy regarding the First Amendment, as well as numerous articles and reports.

The Free Expression Policy Project (FEPP)
170 West Seventy-Sixth St., #301, New York, NY   10023
Web site: www.fepproject.org

Founded in 2000 as a project of the National Coalition Against Censorship, the Free Expression Policy Project (FEPP) has worked to provide research and advocacy on free speech, copyright, and media democracy issues. Specifically, the organization has questioned the value of Internet filters, ratings systems, restrictive copyright laws, mass media consolidation, and censorship undertaken in the name of protecting children and youth. Policy reports and fact sheets addressing these topics and others are available on the organization's Web site.

Media Coalition
275 Seventh Ave., Ste. 1504, New York, NY   10003
(212) 587-4025 • Fax: (212) 587-2436

E-mail: info@mediacoalition.org
Web site: www.mediacoalition.org

The Media Coalition advocates for the preservation of First Amendment rights for all media. Additionally, it defends the right of the American public to access any form of media for communication or entertainment, regardless of whether some people deem the content of that media to be objectionable. To accomplish these goals, the Media Coalition goes to court to challenge laws it sees as unconstitutional and provides regular reports to members of the coalition regarding government activities and legislation relating to the First Amendment.

National Cable & Telecommunications Association (NCTA)
25 Massachusetts Ave. NW, Ste. 100, Washington, DC   20001
(202) 222-2300
Web site: www.ncta.com

The National Cable & Telecommunications Association (NCTA), the cable industry's major trade association, represents the cable operators serving the majority of Americans and provides them with a single, unified voice to address and speak out on issues impacting the industry. The association also works closely with Congress, the executive branch, the courts, and the American public to ensure that public policies dealing with cable television are advanced. Various reports and news releases published by the NCTA can be accessed on its Web site.

National Parent Teacher Association (PTA)
541 N. Fairbanks Ct., Ste. 1300, Chicago, IL   60611
(312) 670-6782 • Fax: (312) 670-6783
E-mail: info@pta.org
Web site: www.pta.org

As the oldest and largest child advocacy organization in the United States, the National Parent Teacher Association (PTA) has worked to ensure that children in America have the opportunity to grow and learn in the most beneficial and appropriate environment possible. While opposed to the originally proposed age-based rating system for television, the PTA helped to develop and continues to support the age-plus-content-based rating system that has been in effect since 1997. *Our Children* is the magazine published by the National PTA, and other reports, surveys, and bulletins can be accessed on the organization's Web site.

Parents Television Council (PTC)
707 Wilshire Blvd., #2075, Los Angeles, CA   90017
(213) 403-1300 • Fax: (213) 403-1301
E-mail: Editor@parentstv.org
Web site: www.parentstv.org

Established originally as a special project of the Media Research Center, the Parents Television Council (PTC) has continued its primary mission of promoting responsible and decent programming in response to the American public's demand for such shows. The PTC publishes the *Family Guide to Prime Time Television* yearly, assessing every sitcom and drama broadcast on the major networks and providing detailed information about their content. Additional publications, such as current television and movie reviews, are available on the organization's Web site.

TV-Turnoff Network
1200 Twenty-Ninth St. NW, Lower Level #1
Washington, DC   20007
(202) 333-9220 • Fax: (202) 333-9221
Web site: www.tvturnoff.org

The TV-Turnoff Network, a national nonprofit organization, believes that if Americans reduced the amount of television they watched, stronger families and communities would result. In order to promote this vision, the organization sponsors National TV-Turnoff Week, during which more than five million people in the United States spend seven days doing anything except watching television. Information about current projects and turnoff weeks can be found on the TV-Turnoff Web site.

Youth Free Expression Network (YFEN)
275 Seventh Ave., 15th Floor, New York, NY   10001
(212) 807-6222 ext. 22 • Fax: (212) 807-6245
Web site: www.ncac.org/YFEN

The Youth Free Expression Network (YFEN), a subgroup of the National Coalition Against Censorship, opposes the censoring of information specifically for young people and promotes free expression for youth. Information detailing the rights of adolescents with regards to the First Amendment is available on the organization's Web site. In addition to providing information, YFEN sponsors workshops and other events to raise awareness and provide solutions to youth censorship at schools and society at large.

Bibliography of Books

Tim Allen and *The Media of Conflict: War Reporting*
Jean Seaton *and Representations of Ethnic Vio-*
lence. New York: Zed Books, 1999.

Bonnie Anderson *News Flash: Journalism, Infotainment*
and the Bottom-Line Business of
Broadcast News. San Francisco:
Jossey-Bass, 2004.

Craig A. *Violent Video Game Effects on Chil-*
Anderson, *dren and Adolescents: Theory, Re-*
Douglas A. *search, and Public Policy.* New York:
Gentile, and Oxford University Press, 2007.
Katherine E.
Buckley

Martin Barker *Ill Effects: The Media/Violence Debate.*
and Julian Petley, New York: Routledge, 1997.
eds.

Karen Boyle *Media and Violence: Gendering the*
Debates. Thousand Oaks, CA: Sage,
2005.

Cynthia Carter *Violence and the Media.* Philadelphia,
PA: Open University Press, 2003.

Cynthia A. *Violence in the Media and Its Influ-*
Cooper *ence on Criminal Defense.* Jefferson,
NC: McFarland & Co., 2007.

Jib Fowles *The Case for Television Violence.*
Thousand Oaks, CA: Sage, 1999.

Jonathan L. *Media Violence and Its Effect on Ag-*
Freedman *gression.* Toronto, Ont: University of
Toronto Press, 2002.

Jeffrey Goldstein, ed.	*Why We Watch: The Attractions of Violent Entertainment*. New York: Oxford University Press, 1998.
Tom Grimes, James A. Anderson	*Media Violence and Aggression: Science and Ideology*. Thousand Oaks, CA: Sage, 2008.
Dave Grossman and Gloria Degaetano	*Stop Teaching Our Kids to Kill: A Call to Action Against TV, Movie and Video Game Violence*. New York: Crown Publishers, 1999.
Gerard Jones	*Killing Monsters: Why Children Need Fantasy, Super Heroes, and Make-Believe Violence*. New York: Basic Books, 2003.
Douglas Kellner	*Media Culture: Cultural Studies, Identity and Politics Between the Modern and the Postmodern*. New York: Routledge, 1995.
Stephen J. Kirsh	*Children, Adolescents, and Media Violence: A Critical Look at the Research*. Thousand Oaks, CA: Sage, 2006.
Lawrence Kutner and Cheryl Olson	*Grand Theft Childhood: The Surprising Truth About Violent Video Games and What Parents Can Do*. New York: Simon & Schuster, 2008.
Joshua Meyrowitz	*No Sense of Place: The Impact of Electronic Media on Social Behavior*. New York: Oxford University Press, 1985.

Hillel Nossek, Annabelle Sreberny, and Prasun Sonwalker, eds. *Media and Political Violence.* Cresskill, NJ: Hapton Press, 2007.

Neil Postman *The Disappearance of Childhood.* New York: Vintage, 1994.

W. James Potter *The 11 Myths of Media Violence.* Thousand Oaks, CA: Sage, 2003.

Thomas Rosenstiel and Amy S. Mitchell *Thinking Clearly: Cases in Journalistic Decision-Making.* New York: Columbia University Press, 2003.

Harold Schechter *Savage Pastimes: A Cultural History of Violent Entertainment.* New York: St. Martin's Press, 2005.

Jean Seaton *Carnage and the Media: The Making and Breaking of News About Violence.* New York: Penguin Books, 2005.

Roger Simpson *Covering Violence: A Guide to Ethical Reporting About Victims & Trauma.* New York: Columbia University Press, 2006.

Karen Sternheimer *It's Not the Media: The Truth About Pop Culture's Influence on Children.* Boulder, CO: Westview, 2003.

James P. Steyer *The Other Parent: The Inside Story of the Media's Effect on Our Children.* New York: Atria, 2002.

David Trend   *The Myth of Media Violence: A Critical Introduction.* Malden, MA: Wiley-Blackwell, 2007.

Index